Praising God Through Prayer and Worship

KAY ARTHUR
PETE De LACY

HARVEST HOUSE PUBLISHERS

EUGENE, OREGON

Cover by Koechel Peterson & Associates, Inc., Minneapolis, Minnesota

PRAISING GOD THROUGH PRAYER AND WORSHIP
Copyright © 2008 by Precept Ministries International
Published by Harvest House Publishers
Eugene, Oregon 97402
www.harvesthousepublishers.com

Library of Congress Cataloging-in-Publication Data
Arthur, Kay, 1933-
Praising God through prayer and worship / Kay Arthur and Pete De Lacy.
   p. cm.—(The new inductive study series)
ISBN-13: 978-0-7369-2304-0 (pbk.)
ISBN-10: 0-7369-2304-7
   1. Bible. O.T. Psalms—Devotional use. 2. God—Worship and love. 3. Worship. 4. Prayer—
Christianity. I. De Lacy, Pete. II. Title.
   BS1430.54.A78 2008
   223'.20071—dc22

                                                2008002134

Printed in the United States of America

08 09 10 11 12 13 14 15 16 / BP-SK / 11 10 9 8 7 6 5 4 3 2

CONTENTS

How to Get Started...

~~~~

Reading directions is sometimes difficult and hardly ever enjoyable! Most often you just want to get started. Only if all else fails will you read the instructions. We understand, but please don't approach this study that way. These brief instructions are a vital part of getting started on the right foot! These few pages will help you immensely.

FIRST

As you study Psalms, you will need four things in addition to this book:

1. A Bible that you are willing to mark in. The marking is essential. An ideal Bible for this purpose is *The New Inductive Study Bible (NISB)*. The *NISB* is in a single-column text format with large, easy-to-read type, which is ideal for marking. The margins of the text are wide and blank for note taking.

The *NISB* also has instructions for studying each book of the Bible, but it does not contain any commentary on the text, nor is it compiled from any theological stance. Its purpose is to teach you how to discern truth for yourself through the inductive method of study. (The various charts and maps that you will find in this study guide are taken from the *NISB*.)

Whichever Bible you use, just know you will need to mark in it, which brings us to the second item you will need…

2. A fine-point, four-color ballpoint pen or various colored fine-point pens that you can use to write in your Bible. Office supply stores should have those.

3. Colored pencils or an eight-color leaded Pentel pencil.

4. A composition book or a notebook for working on your assignments or recording your insights.

SECOND

1. As you study Psalms, you will be given specific instructions for each day's study. These should take you between 20 and 30 minutes a day, but if you spend more time than this, you will increase your intimacy with the Word of God and the God of the Word.

If you are doing this study in a class and you find the lessons too heavy, simply do what you can. To do a little is better than to do nothing. Don't be an all-or-nothing person when it comes to Bible study.

Remember, anytime you get into the Word of God, you enter into more intensive warfare with the devil (our enemy). Why? Every piece of the Christian's armor is related to the Word of God. And our one and only offensive weapon is the sword of the Spirit, which is the Word of God. The enemy wants you to have a dull sword. Don't cooperate! You don't have to!

2. As you read each chapter, train yourself to ask the "5 W's and an H": who, what, when, where, why, and how. Asking questions like these helps you see exactly what the Word of God is saying. When you interrogate the text with the 5 W's and an H, you ask questions like these:

a. **What** is the chapter about?

b. **Who** are the main characters?

c. **When** does this event or teaching take place?

d. **Where** does this happen?

e. **Why** is this being done or said?

f. **How** did it happen?

3. Locations are important in many books of the Bible, so marking references to these in a distinguishable way will be helpful to you. I simply underline every reference to a location in green (grass and trees are green!) using my four-color ballpoint pen. A map is included in this study so you can look up the locations.

4. References to time are also very important and should be marked in an easily recognizable way in your Bible. I mark them by putting a clock like this ⏱ in the margin of my Bible beside the verse where the phrase occurs. You may want to underline or color the references to time in one specific color.

5. You will be given certain key words to mark throughout this study. This is the purpose of the colored pencils and the colored pens. If you will develop the habit of marking your Bible in this way, you will find it will make a significant difference in the effectiveness of your study and in how much you remember.

A **key word** is an important word that the author uses repeatedly in order to convey his message to his readers. Certain key words will show up throughout Psalms; others will be concentrated in a specific psalm. When you mark a key word, you should also mark its synonyms (words that mean the same thing in the context) and any pronouns *(he, his, she, her, it, we, they, us, our, you, their, them)* in the same way you have marked the key word. Also, mark each word the same way in all of its forms (such as *judge*, *judgment*, and *judging*).We will give you suggestions for ways to mark key words in your daily assignments.

You can use colors or symbols or a combination of colors and symbols to mark words for easy identification. However, colors are easier to distinguish than symbols. When we use symbols, we keep them very simple. For example, you could draw a red heart around the word *love* and shade the inside of the heart like this: love .

When marking key words, mark them in a way that is easy for you to remember.

If you devise a color-coding system for marking key words throughout your Bible, then when you look at the pages of your Bible, you will see instantly where a key word is used. You might want to make yourself a bookmark listing the words you mark along with their colors and/or symbols.

6. A PSALMS AT A GLANCE chart is included at the end of this book. As you complete your study of a psalm, record the main theme of that psalm under the appropriate psalm number. The main theme of a psalm is what the psalm deals with the most. It may be a particular subject or teaching.

If you will fill out the PSALMS AT A GLANCE chart as you progress through the study, you will have a synopsis of Psalms when you are finished. If you have a *New Inductive Study Bible,* you will find the same chart in your Bible (page 1014). If you record your themes there, you will have them for a ready reference.

7. Always begin your study with prayer. As you do your part to handle the Word of God accurately, you must remember that the Bible is a divinely inspired book. The words that you are reading are truth, given to you by God so you can know Him and His ways more intimately. These truths are divinely revealed.

For to us God revealed them through the Spirit; for the Spirit searches all things, even the depths of God. For who among men knows the thoughts of a man except the spirit of the man which is in him? Even so the thoughts of God no one knows except the Spirit of God (1 Corinthians 2:10-11).

Therefore ask God to reveal His truth to you as He leads and guides you into all truth. He will if you will ask.

8. Each day when you finish your lesson, meditate on what you saw. Ask your heavenly Father how you should live in light of the truths you have just studied. At times, depending on how God has spoken to you through His Word, you might even want to write LFL ("Lessons for Life") in the margin of your Bible and then, as briefly as possible, record the lesson for life that you want to remember.

THIRD

This study is set up so that you have an assignment for every day of the week—so that you are in the Word daily. If you work through your study in this way, you will find it more profitable than doing a week's study in one sitting. Pacing yourself this way allows time for thinking through what you learn on a daily basis!

The seventh day of each week differs from the other six days. The seventh day is designed to aid group discussion; however, it's also profitable if you are studying this book individually.

The "seventh" day is whatever day in the week you choose to finish your week's study. On this day, you will find a verse or two for you to memorize and STORE IN YOUR HEART. Then there is a passage to READ AND DISCUSS. This will help you focus on a major truth or major truths covered in your study that week.

To assist those using the material in a Sunday school class or a group Bible study, there are Questions for Discussion or Individual Study. Even if you are not doing this study with anyone else, answering these questions would be good for you.

If you are in a group, be sure every member of the class, including the teacher, supports his or her answers and insights from the Bible text itself. Then you will be handling the Word of God accurately. As you learn to see what the text says and compare Scripture with Scripture, the Bible explains itself.

Always examine your insights by carefully observing the text to see what it *says.* Then, before you decide what the passage of Scripture *means,* make sure that you interpret it in the light of its context. Scripture will never contradict Scripture. If it ever seems to contradict the rest of the Word of God, you can be certain that something is being taken out of context. If you come to a passage that is difficult to understand, reserve your interpretations for a time when you can study the passage in greater depth.

The purpose of the Thought for the Week is to share with you what we consider to be an important element in your week of study. We have included it for your evaluation and, hopefully, for your edification. This section will help you see how to walk in light of what you learned.

Books in the New Inductive Study Series are survey courses. If you want to do a more in-depth study of a particular book of the Bible, we suggest you do a Precept Upon Precept Bible study course on that book. You may obtain more information on these courses by contacting Precept Ministries International at 800-763-8280, visiting our website at www.precept.org, or filling out and mailing the response card in the back of this book.

INTRODUCTION TO PSALMS

Man needs to pour out his heart to God, to come before Him and honestly present his concerns and feelings—whether distress or joy, confusion or confidence. Man in right relationship to God was made to sing, to lift up his voice in worship, to speak to God and to others "in psalms and hymns and spiritual songs, singing and making melody with [his] heart to the Lord" (Ephesians 5:19).

That's why some psalms include instructions for accompaniment with stringed instruments or flutes. David, who wrote many of the psalms, appointed Levites to serve in the house of the Lord. Scripture tells us about this transition that followed Israel's wandering: "They ministered with song before the tabernacle of the tent of meeting, until Solomon had built the house of the LORD in Jerusalem" (1 Chronicles 6:31-32).

Psalms is a book of prayer and praise, written by several men inspired by God. The collection of 150 individual psalms is organized into five books. Psalms is not a continuous, chronologically arranged story like we find in the historical books. Unlike prophecy, Psalms has no continuing message developed chronologically or thematically. And unlike epistles (letters), Psalms has no continuous unifying teaching or train of thought throughout the book. The book is an anthology—a collection of 150 different prayers, praises, or songs.

Each psalm is a unit of expression, composed during a moment of need or desire. Each has a unique purpose, although many can be grouped in categories, like the psalms of ascents.

As you study the psalms, remember that they are poems. Hebrew poetry does not contain rhyme and meter like much English poetry. Instead, Hebrew poetry's distinctive feature is parallelism of some form—one line relates to another in various ways. Usually the poetic lines are composed of two (sometimes three) segments in which the second segment repeats, contrasts, or completes the first. Psalms vary in design. Some are acrostics, with each verse or stanza beginning with the next letter from the Hebrew alphabet.

The majority of the psalms have a superscription at the beginning, which designates one or several things: the composer, the occasion, whom it is written for, how it should be accompanied, and what kind of psalm it is. If a psalm has a superscription, read it and consult cross-references noted. This will help you put the psalm into context.

Watch for a theme for each psalm and how it is developed. Sometimes it's stated at the beginning of the psalm, other times in the middle. The theme is the author's design for the psalm (which of course is God's intention).

Some psalms give insights into the history of Israel (such as Psalm 78). Study these carefully. Note the events, God's intervention, and God's watchful care.

Don't miss the central focus of psalms—God. You can learn many things that will lead you to worship and adore Him more. Carefully observe His names, titles, and attributes, and note the believers' *supernatural* response to Him. (You'll also see unbelievers' *natural* responses.)

Don't forget to look for Jesus, who said, "All things which are written about Me in the Law of Moses and the Prophets and the Psalms must be fulfilled" (Luke 24:44).

In a notebook, record your insights about God. As you do this, meditate on what you learn. Spend time in praise and prayer. Let the book of Psalms help you love the Lord your God with all your heart, mind, body, soul, and strength.

Finally, because hymns and contemporary praise music often are based on psalms, when you read words that remind you of a melody, feel free to sing along to God. Pour out your heart to Him as the psalmists did. And listen for His response. Become intimate with God in your prayer and worship.

PSALMS

WHAT WOULD DAVID DO?

Remember the popular question, what would Jesus do? If you study the Gospels, the answer is clear—He would pray early, late, and often. He would cry out to God, confident that God would hear and answer. Was Jesus' prayer life special because He was the Son of God, God made flesh? Yes! Did His pattern reflect the Old Testament, God's Word to mankind in writing? Yes again! The psalms show us how David and others prayed in the millennium before Jesus was born.

DAY ONE

As you read any book of the Bible, you'll see the author emphasize subjects by repeating key words and phrases. Since you'll be marking many of these words and phrases throughout Psalms, a good technique is to record them and how you plan to mark them on a 3 x 5 card and use this as a bookmark. Doing this from psalm to psalm will help you mark consistently and save time.

Read through Psalm 1 (it's only six verses) to see what the

psalm is about. Now read it again, and mark every reference to the *Lord,* including pronouns. To help you get started, we suggest you mark *Lord* with a purple triangle shaded yellow, and mark *blessed* with a purple cloud around it shaded pink. You'll see this second key word over and over in the psalms in other forms (*bless, blessing,* and *blesses*).

Perhaps you noticed the contrast between two kinds of men. Contrasts are usually introduced by the word *but,* so watch for this indicator as you read. You can mark them with a little "lightning bolt" like this: but or a simple slant like this: but.

Read the psalm again, marking *wicked*[1] and its synonyms and also the contrasting *righteous.* You may want to circle *wicked* with a black cloud and write an *R* through *righteous.*

What is the righteous man like? What does he do and not do? What is he compared to?

What is the wicked man like, and what is he compared to? How does this contrast help you understand how God views the two kinds of people? What are the righteous promised?

Which would you rather be? Why?

Determine a theme for this psalm and record it on PSALMS AT A GLANCE, on page 193.

Now let's look at Psalm 2. Mark *nations* and its synonyms, *Lord* (watch for pronouns too), *Son* (read carefully so you catch all the synonyms), and *Zion.* Consider marking *nations* green and underlining it brown. Mark *Lord* as you did in Psalm 1. Before you choose a way to mark *Son,* identify Him. (If you're unsure, read Acts 13:32-33 for a little help.)

Add *nations, Zion,* and *Son* to your bookmark.

What attitude toward God do the nations (the peoples, kings, and rulers) have?

What is God's attitude toward the nations? What evidence does the text give to help you understand why God has this attitude?

Read Micah 4:1-3 to see how the message of Psalm 2:1-4 applies to a prophet in "the last days."

If the nations believed this psalm's truth about the King, what would their attitude be, and how would they act? What does God tell them?

Some classify this as a coronation psalm, written to celebrate the anointing and installation of David or one of his descendants as king. How does Psalm 2 help you see that its powerful truth has a future fulfillment? How does it promise hope for you and me today?

How does this psalm help you pray and worship more intimately?

Finally, determine a theme for this psalm and record it on PSALMS AT A GLANCE.

DAY TWO

Today read Psalm 3 and mark references to the *Lord* and to the psalmist (identified by pronouns such as *I, me,* and *my*). Simply underline or color references to the psalmist. The superscription identifies the author and what his occasion for writing was. For us the issue is not so much what David felt on a specific occasion, but generally how we relate in our circumstances to the cry of the psalmist's heart.

How do you relate to the psalmist's cry? Mark *save* and add it to your bookmark.

What truths about God help you cling to Him in times of distress?

The psalmist cried out for God's blessing on His people (verse 8). During Old Testament times this would probably refer to whom? To whom today? Is there hope for blessing for those who belong to God today?

What time of day does this prayer seem to refer to?

Think on these things and then record a theme for Psalm 3 on PSALMS AT A GLANCE.

Now read Psalm 4 and mark references to the *Lord*. This is a pattern for all the psalms, but we'll keep reminding so you won't forget. Just remember, Beloved of God: Habits are developed by repetition. We hope that by the end of your study of Psalms, this will become your habit for studying the Word.

As in Psalm 3, the psalmist refers to his own condition—things going on around him. Mark references to the psalmist as you did before and take note of his circumstances. Also note the time of day as you did in Psalm 3.

Note the contrast between two kinds of people. Mark *sin* in verse 4 and add it to your bookmark. Throughout the Bible, sin and righteousness are major determinants of man's relationship with God.

Which category does the psalmist put himself in? Do you identify with him? Can you turn this psalm into your own prayer before you go to bed tonight?

Finally, record a theme for Psalm 4 on PSALMS AT A GLANCE.

DAY THREE

Read Psalm 5 and note the psalmist's purpose for writing and the timing. Now read it again and mark references to the *Lord*, the psalmist, and his enemies. Add *sing*[2] and *lovingkindness*[3] to your bookmark and mark them in this psalm. *Lovingkindness* describes covenant love, steadfast and merciful. Also mark *iniquity*[4] and *transgression*,[5] synonyms for *sin*. Although there are sometimes slight distinctions in meaning in the Hebrew, they're minor and infrequent enough for us to mark these words the same way for now. Add these to your bookmark because you'll see them over and over in Psalms.

What characteristics of the Lord do you see in this psalm? How do they compare with what you learned in the first four psalms? The psalms are so rich in describing God and His works, you might enjoy journaling what you learn about Him from psalm to psalm. It's early enough in the study so if you want to do this, go back to day 1 and compile into one list what you've seen so far. Add what you learn from each of the remaining 145 psalms.

What is God's attitude toward wickedness in all its forms? What contrast do you see between sinful behavior and what God is like? Notice that the contrast is not between David's enemies and himself, but between his enemies and God. What does this tell you about David?

How does David's example contrast with the way people relate to God today? How do you relate to Him?

Determine a theme for Psalm 5 on PSALMS AT A GLANCE.

DAY FOUR

Read Psalm 6 without stopping to mark anything. What kind of psalm is this? What does the psalmist ask for? Verse 2 says his "bones are dismayed,"[6] and he asks to be healed. What seems to be his problem? How does verse 2 relate to verse 1?

Again, read and mark references to the *Lord* and the psalmist, and add to your journal about God.

When David asks for healing, does he appeal to his character or God's? What characteristics does David appeal to?

Lovingkindness (verse 4) is a characteristic of God we see throughout the Bible. The word is translated from the Hebrew *chesed,* a covenant term.

Observe the verb tenses in verses 8 and 9. "Has heard" in English implies action already completed. What does this tell you about David's confidence in prayer? Do you have this confidence? If not, our prayer for you is that by the end of this study of psalms you will gain this intimacy and confidence in prayer and worship that David had toward God.

Don't forget to record a theme for Psalm 6 on PSALMS AT A GLANCE.

DAY FIVE

Read Psalm 7 today, marking *Lord, sing, praise, righteousness,*[7] *wicked,* and *judgment.* Add the new key words to your bookmark. You'll find *sing, praise,* and *thanks* throughout the psalms.

Now, what did you see regarding justice for the righteous and his enemies? What conditions bring judgment? What brings vindication? What characteristic of God is the basis for just judgment?

What did you learn about God to take to heart today, to trust in as David the psalmist did?

Finally, determine a theme for Psalm 7 and record it on PSALMS AT A GLANCE.

DAY SIX

Get ready to sing today, Beloved. Read the first and last

verses of Psalm 8 and mark repeated phrases that remind you of praise choruses or songs.

Now read the whole psalm, marking references to *God* and *man*. Then list everything you learn about God and man in these nine verses.

What do you see about yourself in relation to God? How will you respond to God today in worship in light of this truth?

Finally, determine a theme for Psalm 8 and record it on PSALMS AT A GLANCE.

DAY SEVEN

 Store in your heart: Psalm 5:3
Read and discuss: Psalms 1–8

QUESTIONS FOR DISCUSSION OR INDIVIDUAL STUDY

- What situations in the psalmist's life caused him to cry out to God?

- What did you learn about God's character and ways in these psalms?

- What did you learn about the relationship between God and the nations—those who do not obey Him?

- Do these psalms give you patterns for prayer— when to pray, why to pray, and how to pray?

- Summarize the message of these psalms—share what you put on PSALMS AT A GLANCE.

- What message of hope do these psalms give?

ം What applications can you make to your own life?

ം How does this week's study motivate you to pray?

THOUGHT FOR THE WEEK

Psalm 5:3 says, "In the morning, O LORD, You will hear my voice; in the morning I will order my prayer to You and eagerly watch." Oh, that we would eagerly watch for God's answer. What a great example! Think about this: Every morning when you wake up, lift your voice to God in prayer for that day. Then eagerly watch through the day to see His answers. Wow! Wouldn't you like to have that reliance on God? Maybe you already do.

Cultivating this intimacy with God takes time and practice. It's developed over a lifetime of various circumstances. Wherever you are in your walk with God, whatever He has taken you through, He is always there. His lovingkindness and mercies are new every morning. He never abandons you.

The superscriptions of Psalms 3 through 8 tell us David wrote them. Even if you haven't studied 2 Samuel and 1 Chronicles to learn about David, you can learn volumes about his life from the way he prays and the things he prays for.

How about you? If people overheard you praying, would they know about your life, about what's going on? Would they learn about your daily needs, wants, and fears, as well as the reasons for your confidence?

What would your prayer life reveal about your relationship to God? If you made a list of what you asked Him for, what you said to Him, and how you praised Him for what He has done and will do, would people know you worship God?

And if people wrote down your prayers for a day, would they get the idea that you truly rely on God? After all, in these first eight psalms we've already seen prayer in the morning and evening, on arising and retiring. When do you pray?

We've asked these questions to cause you to take stock, to start to measure your own intimacy with God in prayer and worship. The Word of God will do its work as you continue through the psalms. It will lay bare things that need healing, but it will also give you encouragement and hope.

As we spend a lifetime praying, we gain more and more confidence and more and more intimacy with God from our eager watchfulness for His answers. Often we think of prayer as communicating *to* God, talking *to* or *with* Him, and our Bible reading and study as hearing *from* God. Both are true. If we don't apprehend these two functions properly, our intimacy with God won't grow as deep as it should.

Prayer is indeed talking to God and answers are God speaking back to us. Answers may come right away or be delayed. We may need a season of prayer before we receive an answer, and Scripture emphasizes persevering prayer. But God does speak back to us.

Bible reading and study is clearly hearing from God, but we must come before Him in prayer before we begin because spiritual things are spiritually discerned (1 Corinthians 2:13-15). We ask our resident Teacher, the Holy Spirit, to open the eyes of our understanding. The insight into Scripture that He gives is the answer to prayer.

Psalm 1:2 points to this twofold approach to God. It describes the man who is blessed: "But his delight is in the law of the LORD, and in His law he meditates day and night." Prayer and Bible reading and study go hand in hand in our communication with God—a growing intimacy that helps us worship Him in all we do.

HEAR A JUST CAUSE

"Hear a just cause, O LORD, give heed to my cry; give ear to my prayer, which is not from deceitful lips" (Psalm 17:1). David knows God judges justly, and he cries out to Him on that basis. He fully trusts God's decisions. He knows his God and is confident his God knows him. Do you? Can you honestly say you *run* to God, trusting Him?

DAY ONE

Read Psalm 9 today. Remember, each psalm contains truth about God and our relationship to Him. Each has its own purpose, and each is worthy of meditation. Take your time. As you read, mark references to *God* and to the psalmist as we've been doing. Mark *salvation* as you marked *save* in Psalm 3 and add it to your bookmark.

Now, let's look at this psalm one section at a time. What repeated phrase do you see in verses 1 and 2? Mark it. What do you learn about the psalmist? Do you do what he does and feel the way he feels about God?

Read verses 3-6 and mark *judging, wicked,* and *righteously* as we've marked similar words before. What did you learn about God?

Read verses 7-10 and mark *judgment.* What do you learn about God and judgment?

Now read verses 11-16. What contrast do you see between the way God treats the nations and the way He treats the afflicted? How does this help you today? Mark *blood* and add it to your bookmark. Requiring blood involves justice; *requires* is translated *avenges* in many translations.

Read verses 17-20 and mark *nations.* How do these verses parallel what you saw in previous sections? What is the bottom-line truth about God and judgment in Psalm 9?

Finally, determine a theme for Psalm 9 and record it on PSALMS AT A GLANCE on page 193.

DAY TWO

We continue with judgment psalms today. Read Psalm 10, marking references to *God* and the *wicked* as usual.

Now, what did you learn about the wicked? What do they think of God? From all you listed about God, including what you learned this week and last, what do you think about the man who thinks like this?

What does the psalmist call on God to do? What's the reason for this cry to God? What verses do you see this in? What will God do for the humble, the orphan, and the oppressed?

From the context of the entire psalm, who is the "man who is of the earth" in verse 18?

Finally, determine a theme for Psalm 10 and record it on PSALMS AT A GLANCE.

DAY THREE

Read Psalm 11 and mark references to the *Lord,* the *righteous,* and the *wicked.* Watch for synonymous phrases like *the upright in heart.* This short psalm is packed with truth so take your time, meditate on what you see, and tuck these truths in your heart for the future. Call on them when you feel the way David did.

Now, what is the attitude of...

∞ the wicked toward the righteous?

∞ the Lord toward the wicked?

∞ the Lord toward the righteous?

∞ the righteous toward the Lord?

What did you learn about the Lord that you can trust in today and tomorrow, Beloved?

Determine a theme for Psalm 11 and record it on PSALMS AT A GLANCE.

Now read Psalm 12. Note the parallelism in verse 1. What is David's cry about? What is his concern?

Read through the psalm again, marking references to the *Lord,* the *godly,* and those who are not godly. Look for pronouns that refer to these people.

What are some characteristics of the ungodly?

What's the contrast between the words of the sons of men and the words of the Lord? Read James 3:1-12. What kinds of words should come from our mouths? How will you apply this truth to your life this week?

Finally, record a theme for Psalm 12 on PSALMS AT A GLANCE.

DAY FOUR

Read Psalm 13 today, again marking references to God. Also mark *rejoice* and key repeated phrases that reveal the main idea of this psalm. Then ask and answer as many of the 5 W's and an H as you can. For example, how does David feel? What does he ask for? What does he say he has done and will do?

Then think about yourself. Do you cry to God with the same passion? Do you trust Him the way David did?

Now read Psalm 14, marking the key words on your bookmark. Also mark references to the nation *Israel*. Mark *fool*, but don't add it to your bookmark; it's used in only a few more psalms.

Now, compare verses 1-3 with Romans 3:10-12. What did you learn?

What is David's hope? In David's time, Israel wasn't in captivity, right? So what do you think "When the LORD restores His captive people" refers to?

Record themes for Psalms 13 and 14 on PSALMS AT A GLANCE.

DAY FIVE

Read Psalm 15 and mark the key words on your bookmark. What great question does this psalm ask? What do "abide in Your tent" and "dwell on Your holy hill" mean?

List the answer to David's question point by point as he records it.

Now measure yourself against the standard David gives us in this psalm.

Now read Psalm 16. Mark the key words from your book-mark.

What does David ask God to do? What is the basis of his request? Answer right from the text. (Hint: It's what David knows about God.)

Paul quotes verse 10 in Acts 13:35 as he preaches about Jesus in the synagogue of Pisidian Antioch. Read Acts 13:32-39 for the context of his use of this verse. Luke, writing Acts under the inspiration of the Holy Spirit, shows that Paul attributed Psalm 16:10 to Jesus, not David. We don't know how David understood this psalm, but we do know that *God* intended it to be a prophecy about Jesus!

Record themes for Psalms 15 and 16 on PSALMS AT A GLANCE.

DAY SIX

We'll wrap this week up with just one psalm today, Psalm 17. As usual, read and mark key words and phrases from your bookmark. This psalm contrasts the wicked and righteous as we've seen other psalms do.

What does David ask for, and on what basis does he trust God to give him his request?

Did you catch the familiar phrase "apple of the eye"? Now you know where it originated! Here David asks God to keep him as "the apple of the eye." His son Solomon uses the phrase for teaching that a father wants his son to keep his teaching as "the apple of [his] eye." The prophet Zechariah describes Israel as "the apple of [God's] eye." And we use it today. "Apple" of course refers to the pupil—the center of the eye, the part you look through to focus on some object. We are blessed to be the apple of God's eye—the very focal point of His sight.

What other requests from this psalm would you like to make to God?

Record a theme for Psalm 17 on PSALMS AT A GLANCE.

DAY SEVEN

Store in your heart: Psalm 17:8

Read and discuss: Psalms 9–17

QUESTIONS FOR DISCUSSION OR INDIVIDUAL STUDY

- What's going on in the psalmist's life that causes him to cry out to God in these psalms?

- What did you learn about God's character and ways in these psalms?

- What did you learn about the relationship between God and the wicked—those who don't obey him?

- How do key concepts in these psalms compare with those in last week's? Did you learn any new concepts?

- Do these psalms reveal patterns for prayer—what to pray for, whom and what to trust in, or how to pray?

- Summarize the message of these psalms; share what you put on PSALMS AT A GLANCE.

- What message of hope do these psalms give?

- What can you apply to your own life? What specific verses do you want to recall and apply this week?

- How does this week's study motivate you to pray?

THOUGHT FOR THE WEEK

As I studied Psalms 9 through 17, I reviewed and recited the attributes of God they declare. I meditated on them, thought carefully about them—calmly, seriously, and for some time. That's what I urge you to do, Beloved, day after day. Let them linger in your memory.

God reveals Himself to us in His holy Word, the Bible, the Old Testament and New. As Psalm 12:6 says, "The words of the LORD are pure words, as silver tried in a furnace on the earth, refined seven times." So when we speak God's Word in song or prayer, or when we even think it, we reflect His glorious character back to Him as in a mirror of silver refined seven times. We know from His righteous character (what He is) that He judges righteously (what He does). As David says, He will vindicate you and me according to our righteousness and integrity (Psalm 7:8).

But this righteousness is not our own in any self-made sense. David writes elsewhere that the Lord's righteousness is the basis for acquittal (Psalm 35:24), revival (143:11), and answers to prayer (143:1). And the Old Testament generally points to that *objective* righteousness coming in the Messiah, as Jeremiah so eloquently prophesies: "The LORD our righteousness" (Jeremiah 23:6).

That righteousness came as predicted: "But by His doing you are in Christ Jesus, who became to us wisdom from God, and righteousness and sanctification, and redemption" (1 Corinthians 1:30).

Because I believe the gospel of Jesus Christ—that Jesus died for my sins, paying the debt I owe, and rose from the dead, ascending into heaven to the right hand of the Father—I have eternal life. When God looks at me, He sees Christ's righteousness imputed to me. He doesn't see my self-made righteousness "like a filthy garment" (Isaiah 64:6); He sees

His Son's pure and holy righteousness. Jesus was the perfectly obedient Son, the Lamb of God, our Passover that was slain. Because the Father sees that righteousness, He vindicates me from the accusations the father of lies, the devil, spouts out.

God is my shield. He saves the upright in heart.

This is incredible! "When I consider Your heavens, the work of Your fingers, the moon and the stars which You have ordained," like David I ask, "What is man that You take thought of him, and the son of man that You care for Him?" (Psalm 8:3-4). *Who am I, Lord, that You take thought of me, that You care for me?*

Here we are, lower than the angels yet knowing that God will crown us with glory and majesty. God, who has a majestic name, crowns us with His majesty, giving us a share of Jesus' glory by naming us Christians ("little Christs"). He has made us in His image, to rule over His creation, the works of His hands, all sheep and oxen, the beasts of the field, the birds of the heavens, and the fish of the sea. "O LORD, our LORD, how majestic is Your name in all the earth!"

Our proper response? With David, "I will give thanks to the LORD with all my heart. I will tell of Your wonders. I will be glad and exult in You; I will sing praise to Your name, O Most High" (Psalm 9:1-2).

As for me, I will remember that God is in His holy temple, on His throne in heaven, and that His eyes see and test the hearts of men. I will remember that He loves righteousness and that if my heart is upright, He will know and see it. He will judge righteously—He will distinguish between the wicked and the righteous even when men don't. When wickedness prevails in the affairs of men, when men pervert justice by letting the wicked go unpunished and free, I know that He will judge surely and righteously. In the end, His justice will prevail, and in that I trust.

These psalms are God's words, pure as silver refined seven times. By His Word God preserves those who love Him, today and forever. My task is simply to bless God, trust Him, and wait. I don't know how long—His righteous judgments may take a long time by my reckoning and according to the number of my days, but not long by God's reckoning, His view of time.

In Him I trust. And wait expectantly, hopefully, rejoicing.

SOME BOAST IN HORSES

ᘒ ᘒ ᘒ ᘒ

Whom or what do you trust? Horses and chariots are not common sights today, but they were in David's time. What are their equivalents today? What things of men do we sometimes put our trust in instead of God? Think about these this week, Beloved, as we study four psalms that instruct us in trust.

DAYS ONE, TWO, & THREE

We'll take three days to look at Psalm 18 because it's 50 verses long. Your first task is to read through the entire psalm. Then read 2 Samuel 22 and compare the two. Don't compare word for word (they're not identical); instead, compare basic concepts and messages. What do you see?

Second Samuel 22:1 tells us when David wrote the psalm—after he was delivered from Saul and his enemies. Unlike other psalms written during Saul's persecution of David, this one is written much later, during David's reign as king and long after Saul's death. David now has peace from his enemies, and he's recapping what God has done for him.

Now read through Psalm 18 again and mark the key words from your bookmark.

Now go through the psalm paragraph by paragraph and note what each group of verses is about. For example, what's the main subject of verses 1-6? Then look at verses 7-15. Different translations parse the paragraphs differently (they're man-made), but using what you have in your Bible, summarize each paragraph in a few words.

When you've completed this, look at what you've recorded and summarize what David said about God and what God did for him. Note David's responsive actions toward God because of what God did for him. Is God the same today as in David's times? Does He do the same for you? Do you respond to God the way David did?

Record your theme for Psalm 18 on PSALMS AT A GLANCE.

DAY FOUR

Just one Psalm today: 19, and all in one day. Read it and mark the key words from your bookmark. Add *Redeemer* to your bookmark—the first use of this term in Psalms. It will appear many times later, showing this truth about God is important throughout Psalms.

Now compare Psalm 19:1-6 to Romans 1:18-20. What do you see?

As we did for Psalm 18, look at each paragraph and record what each tells us. How does God communicate with man about Himself according to verses 1-6? How does He communicate to man about Himself according to verses 7-10?

Finally, what does God do according to verses 11-14?

Does verse 14 sound familiar?

Finally, record a theme for Psalm 19 on PSALMS AT A GLANCE.

DAY FIVE

Read Psalm 20, marking key words as usual.

Make a list of everything David asks the Lord to do. Almost all his requests start with *may*.

What is David's confidence? The Hebrew word translated *boast* in the NASB literally means "to bring to mind" or "remember" and is translated *trust* in most other translations. But here, in the context of verses 6-9, what's the idea we're to grasp?

Finally, record a theme for Psalm 20 on PSALMS AT A GLANCE.

DAY SIX

Today read Psalm 21. Mark the key words from your bookmark as usual. Note that the king is David.

Compare Psalm 20:6-9 with Psalm 21:1. What ideas connect the two psalms?

Note what you learn about God and David. Then ask yourself if you trust in God as David did.

Finally, record a theme for Psalm 21 on PSALMS AT A GLANCE.

DAY SEVEN

 Store in your heart: Psalm 20:7

Read and discuss: Psalms 18–21

QUESTIONS FOR DISCUSSION OR INDIVIDUAL STUDY

∾ What is going on in the psalmist's life that causes him to cry out to God in these psalms?

∾ What did you learn about God's character and ways in these psalms?

∾ Compare and contrast the key concepts in these psalms with those you studied last week. What did you learn that's new?

∾ Do these psalms give you patterns for prayer—what to pray for, what to trust in, and how to pray?

∾ Summarize the message of these psalms—share what you put on PSALMS AT A GLANCE.

∾ What message of hope does God give you in these psalms?

∾ What can you apply to your life? What verses spoke to your heart that you want to recall this week?

∾ How does this week's study motivate you to pray and worship God obediently?

THOUGHT FOR THE WEEK

Some trust in horses. Until the early twentieth century, biblical references to horses made perfect sense to most people. They were *the* primary source of transportation. Horses carried people, pulled wagons and carts, and plowed. People knew their horses. Some knew their boats, and steam had been harnessed, so sailing gave way to "getting up a head of steam" for both ships and railroad locomotives. But horses were still common.

Today most of us in the industrialized nations know cars, trucks, and airplanes. Petroleum powers our lives. But the underlying biblical principle is the same regardless of the kind of power that enables us to travel and work. We have a choice—to trust God's sovereignty or man's creations.

Oh yes, man's creations are fueled by God's creation: the wind, the heating of water to produce steam, the refining of crude oil to produce fuels, and a host of man's other discoveries about the world God created. But the question is, what do we trust? Do we trust created man's ingenuity to harness the rest of creation, or do we trust the Creator Himself?

In Romans 1, Paul lays out a fundamental truth that is at the heart of trust and worship. He teaches that although God made Himself known through creation, man worshipped the creature rather than the Creator. You probably don't carve idols and worship them, but do you put your trust in man's ingenuity and creations?

It's easy to do all the time. Every time we flip a light switch, we trust man's ingenuity to make light. When we fly in an airplane, we trust man's ingenuity to engineer and build a craft to take us off the ground and get us back down safely. We trust science, engineering, and other human disciplines for our everyday lives.

God wants us to acknowledge that He is behind all of man's projects and controls the outcomes. He is in charge; He should be trusted. Whenever we have a situation, He commands us to turn to Him first and give Him glory in the end. He wants us to acknowledge privately and publicly that He has all power and knowledge, and He is prepared to grant us what we ask.

Then He wants us to sing to Him and praise Him for His power. He calls us to return His blessing, to bless Him, praising Him and rejoicing in Him for His goodness toward us.

So! Shall we boast in horses and chariots or praise God as David did?

THE LORD IS MY SHEPHERD

~~~~~

Sometimes biblical metaphors are difficult to understand. Most of us have no firsthand experience with sheep. But David's audience did, and so did Jesus'. They understood *shepherd*—the noun and the verb. For the most part our environment doesn't include shepherds and sheep, but we can understand affliction and suffering, feeling alone and abandoned, crying out to God in desperate times. Some things are easy to identify with, and that's the purpose of the psalms— they help us identify with the psalmist's cry to God.

DAYS ONE & TWO

David wrote Psalm 22 to describe how he felt in a particular situation, but the psalm also prophesies the death of Jesus Christ on the cross. Jesus quoted the first phrase of the first verse in Matthew 27:46 and Mark 15:34. Some believe that speaking the first line of any psalm was equivalent to invoking the entire psalm. The Gospels don't record Jesus quoting other parts of the psalm, so we don't know if He did.

We'll compare each verse with similar New Testament verses, and you can decide.

Read Psalm 22, marking references to *God*.

Now read the following Gospel accounts of the crucifixion and see if you can match parts of them with parts of Psalm 22:

- ∾ Matthew 27:38-46

- ∾ Mark 15:22-37

- ∾ Luke 23:33-46

- ∾ John 19:17-37

Now read Hebrews 2:9-12 and Revelation 19:5 and compare them to Psalm 22.

Whether David is speaking of his own situation or prophetically speaking of Jesus, what is the outcome? When someone is in the dire straits described in verses 1-18, what does Psalm 22:19-31 promise?

Record a theme for Psalm 22 on PSALMS AT A GLANCE.

DAY THREE

Now we come to the most famous psalm, the one most often memorized and read in times of trouble. Perhaps you can recite it. Read Psalm 23 and mark all references to *God*.

For further study of this psalm, we highly recommend *A Shepherd Looks at Psalm 23* by Phillip Keller, who powerfully brings to light features of shepherds and shepherding relevant to our lives. In our brief survey of this psalm, we can only highlight these features and leave it to you for deeper study. Here's a brief synopsis of what the good shepherd does:

∾ lovingly takes care of his sheep

∾ ensures that they have food, water, rest, and safe paths to walk on

∾ protects them from dangers in the wilderness, particularly predators that would attack, kill, and devour them

∾ carries a rod and a staff to protect the sheep and to herd them

∾ drives away annoying and dangerous insects by putting oil in the sheep's noses

Read John 10:1-16. How does Psalm 23 help you understand your relationship to Jesus?

Now read Psalm 24 and mark references to *God* and other key words from your bookmark. How does this psalm describe God? Who may ascend to the hill of the Lord (approach God)?

What do we know about the King of glory? (You may want to color this phrase throughout this psalm.) Who is this King of glory?

Record themes for Psalms 23 and 24 on PSALMS AT A GLANCE.

DAY FOUR

Read through Psalm 25 and mark key words as usual. Mark *covenant,* used for the first time in the psalms here. Add it to your bookmark. *Covenant* is a key word throughout the Bible—God is a covenant keeper. So paying attention to *covenant* is important not only in Psalms but in every book of the Bible. One way to mark it is to shade it red (for blood) and outline it in yellow.

Now, what did you learn about God? What does David ask God to do for him?

List everything you learn about the Lord's lovingkindness and covenant. Remember that *lovingkindness* is a covenant term, so these ideas are related.

Finally, don't forget to record a theme for Psalm 25 on PSALMS AT A GLANCE.

DAY FIVE

Read Psalm 26 today, once again marking key words from your bookmark. Add *love* and *hate*.[8] You can mark *love* with a red heart and mark *hate* with a black heart or a red heart with a slash through it.

What is David's attitude toward himself in this psalm? Whom does he contrast himself to? What does he ask God for and why?

Compare David's use of *Redeemer* in this psalm with his use in Psalms 19 and 25. What did you learn?

What is David's attitude toward God? What does David say he loves and hates?

Record a theme for Psalm 26 on PSALMS AT A GLANCE.

DAY SIX

Our last Psalm for this week is 27. Read it today, marking the key words from your bookmark. Make sure to mark the references to the *tabernacle*,[9] *tent,* and *house of the Lord.*

Compare Psalm 27:4-6 to Psalm 26:8. What do you see?

Now a few historical facts. There was no temple in Jerusalem in David's day; his son Solomon built it during his reign. So from Israel's time at Mount Sinai until the dedication of this temple, Israel worshipped at the tabernacle, the tent God dwelt in among them. Even after David brought the tabernacle from Kiriath-jearim to Jerusalem, the ark of the covenant resided in a tent, and Israel met God there. How does this help you understand verses 4-6?

Recording what David says about the Lord is important. It's also important to see what David asks for and how he asks.

Finally, record a theme for Psalm 27 on PSALMS AT A GLANCE.

DAY SEVEN

 Store in your heart: Psalm 23

Read and discuss: Psalms 22-23

QUESTIONS FOR DISCUSSION OR INDIVIDUAL STUDY

- ∾ What did you learn about God's shepherding? Review Psalm 23 line by line.

- ∾ What importance does Psalm 23 have for your life? Can you share a time when it gave you great comfort?

- ∾ Share how you relate to walking in the valley of the shadow of death.

- ∾ What is David referring to when he mentions the Lord's rod and staff? How has God comforted you with His rod and staff?

- ∾ What does "dwell in the house of the LORD" mean?

∾ Recite Psalm 23 together to close this part of your discussion.

∾ Discuss the parallels between Psalm 22 and Jesus' crucifixion.

∾ How do you see this psalm fitting into Jesus' cry from the cross?

∾ What can you apply to your life from Psalm 22? If you are able, discuss a time when you believed God abandoned you. How does Psalm 23 help you reinterpret that situation?

THOUGHT FOR THE WEEK

One of the best-known scriptures is Psalm 23. I remember memorizing it as a child. I remember it being recited at funerals. Not that I understood its power or even believed it was true about my relationship to God—and it wasn't because I was lost. I wasn't a sheep in the Good Shepherd's flock. I was in the flock of the enemy.

Since I've been redeemed and have the Lord as my shepherd, I've gained a new perspective. I've studied sheep and now know that I need a Shepherd who takes care of me. Regardless of how independently I act, I'm truly dependent. I need God to lead me to green pastures and not to attempt to feed on the world's dry ones. I need quiet waters to still my soul, to give me peace in this tumultuous and noisy world. It's hard to get away to be quiet. There's too much noise and "stuff" going on. I need the Shepherd to restore my soul.

Maybe you feel this way too. It may be hard for you to get away from it all, to get quiet before the Lord, to tune out the noise of the world. Maybe you need to find that quiet time and place when and where you can refocus—a real Sabbath, a real vacation, a real place of retreat and renewal. It's time for us to get away and spend quiet time in the Word, eating from the table God sets before us in His Word, listening for His voice.

If your life is filled with circumstances that prevent you from getting away like this, what do you do? How do you find that time and place of rest and renewal? You set aside a quiet time! Sometime during the day amid intense surroundings you need to find a haven, to carve out a time and space to read the Word and listen quietly for the Shepherd's voice.

This may sound idealistic, but it's so necessary to find a quiet time alone with God. Certainly each of the psalms in this week's lesson has something you identify with, something that resonates with your life today. It may be something you are experiencing right now or something your heart desires for the future. Either way, talk to God about it today. And when you can't find the words, let the psalms help you. David and the other psalmists have so eloquently recorded their hearts' cries that just reading them with the same heart-felt passion will help you.

Lift up your soul to God. Trust Him to give you peace and answers to your cry. Remember His covenant promises and lovingkindness. Remember your redemption, your salvation. Tell Him how much you love Him and want to be with Him. He'll honor that! No parents tire of hearing their children say they love them.

God understands you and hears you and never ever grows weary of you calling Him.

His Favor Is
for a Lifetime

How permanent is the love of God? How long does His anger last? How sure can we be of this? And how long should we be thankful to God for what He has done for us? As you study Psalms 28–34 this week, watch for references to time that help you answer these questions.

DAY ONE

We're going to cover two short but very different psalms today. Start by reading Psalm 28, marking the key words from your bookmark. Verse four uses the words *requite*[10] and *recompense*,[11] which may not be familiar to you. There's not much difference between the two; both essentially mean to pay what's due.

Now, how does David view God? What does he ascribe to God?

Note the last line of the psalm. What other psalm does this allude to?

Now read Psalm 29, marking the key words from your

bookmark. What key repeated phrase do you see? Underline or color this phrase in Psalm 29.

What is the main idea of this psalm?

How does David view God in this psalm? List these in your notebook. Do you view God the same way David did?

How are Psalms 28 and 29 different? How are they similar?

Finally, remember to determine themes for these two psalms and record them on PSALMS AT A GLANCE.

DAY TWO

The superscription to Psalm 30 says it's a song at the dedication of the house and also a psalm of David. This must refer to David's own house, not the house of the Lord (the temple) because Solomon dedicated the temple after David died.

Read Psalm 30, marking the key words from your bookmark. Include references to time as usual.

What is David thankful for? What has God done for him? List these in your notebook, and consider if you have the same things to be thankful for. Has God done any of these things for you?

Finally, determine a theme for Psalm 30 and record it on PSALMS AT A GLANCE.

DAY THREE

Read Psalm 31 and mark the key words from your bookmark. From your markings, list what you learned about God—His character and ways (actions).

Now read the psalm again and underline each thing

David asks God to do for him. In another color underline or highlight what David says he does and will do. Have you ever asked God to do these things for you?

What attributes of God does David appeal to for his help? Do *you* trust these qualities of God? Maybe you've never thought about these before, but when things aren't going well (and normal Christian life includes trials), do you feel like David, who reveals his innermost self? And like him, do you trust God's character—holy, omnipotent, just, and merciful?

Finally, determine a theme for Psalm 31 and record it on PSALMS AT A GLANCE.

DAY FOUR

Read Psalm 32 today. Mark the key words and phrases from your bookmark plus others that seem to be key to the meaning of this psalm.

One way to think through a psalm is to note what each paragraph teaches. The NASB divides Psalm 32 into three paragraphs: verses 1-2, 3-7, and 8-11. Notice how different the contents of each are though they're also contextually related (connected). How are the first two paragraphs related?

Now, read 1 John 1:9 and compare it to Psalm 32:3-7. What do you see?

Who is speaking in verses 8-9? Who is addressed? Why? In other words, how does this relate to verses 1-7?

Who is speaking or writing in verses 10-11? How do these verses relate to verses 1-2?

Now determine a theme for Psalm 32 and record it on PSALMS AT A GLANCE.

DAY FIVE

Read Psalm 33 and mark the key words from your bookmark.

How does the first verse of Psalm 33 relate to the last verse of Psalm 32? (Psalm 33 doesn't have a superscription ascribing this psalm to David, but does it sound like him?)

List the ways this psalm tells us to praise the Lord.

According to this psalm, why should we praise the Lord?

The first line of verse 12 may be familiar to you: "Blessed is the nation whose God is the LORD." Maybe you've heard a sermon or teaching on it. What is the context of the entire verse? Just from the text and the context, what nation is this verse about?

What relationship between the psalmist and God do you see in verses 18-22? Is this *your* relationship with God?

Finally, determine a theme for Psalm 33 and record it on PSALMS AT A GLANCE.

DAY SIX

As our last psalm for the week, read Psalm 34, marking the key words from your bookmark and others you observe in this psalm. Remember to mark all time references.

Whom does David call to exalt the Lord with him? Does this include you?

According to verse 4, how did God respond to David's cry to Him? Who are "they" in verse 5?

Again, a paragraph-by-paragraph analysis of this psalm will help you walk through it. Just list in the margin of your Bible or in your notebook what each paragraph is about and then see how they relate.

Finally, determine a theme for Psalm 34 and record it on
PSALMS AT A GLANCE.

DAY SEVEN

 Store in your heart: Psalm 34:7-8
Read and discuss: Psalms 29–30; 32; 34; 1 John 1:9

QUESTIONS FOR DISCUSSION OR INDIVIDUAL STUDY

- Discuss what you learned about the attributes of God
  in these psalms.

- What interaction between David and God do you
  see? In what ways is your prayer life like David's?

- Compare how you hear the voice of God to Psalm
  29. Do you ever say, "Glory!"

- Share a time in your life that parallels the mourning,
  weeping, and rejoicing David mentioned in Psalm 30.

- Discuss 1 John 1:9 and Psalm 32. How does this
  apply to you? Can you relate to the way David felt
  before and after he confessed his sin?

- What do you think and feel when you read, "The
  angel of the LORD encamps around those who fear
  Him, and rescues them"?

- What is "the fear of the LORD" according to Psalm
  34? What does it offer those who fear Him? How
  and where do we learn the fear of God?

- What is your favorite verse from this week, and how
  did it minister to you? Besides the ones you were

asked to memorize, what one verse grabbed your attention the most?

THOUGHT FOR THE WEEK

[God's] anger is but for a moment,
His favor is for a lifetime;
Weeping may last for the night,
But a shout of joy comes in the morning.
      (Psalm 30:5)

David believed these truths as much as anyone. The superscription says that David wrote this psalm for the dedication of his house, but check out its relevancy to an incident that occurred in 2 Samuel 12.

David committed adultery with Bathsheba and tried to cover it up. When that plan failed, he ordered Joab to send her husband, Uriah, into fierce fighting that killed him. David committed murder using the sword of the Ammonites and then took Bathsheba as his wife.

When Nathan the prophet confronted David, he asked David why he had despised the Word of the Lord by doing this evil. Then Nathan prophesied three consequences David would receive for his sins: no end to war in his house, his wives sleeping publicly with other men, and the death of his child born to Bathsheba.

David fasted and prayed for seven days, begging God to spare the baby. When the child died, he got up, washed, worshipped, and ate. Later, Bathsheba conceived Solomon, who succeeded David as king.

With that background, think of the things David wrote in Psalm 30 about how long God's anger lasts and how long His favor lasts. If one consequence of David's sin would last his entire life—"the sword shall never depart from your house"

(2 Samuel 12:10)—how could David say God's anger lasts a moment and His favor a lifetime?

The answer is that David's entire life truly was a moment compared with eternity! When David died, his wars and the evil from his own house both ended. Solomon ruled in peace. David saw the morning after his child died and he saw an eternity of joy ahead with his God. He said he would give thanks to God forever.

> How blessed is he whose transgression
>   is forgiven,
> Whose sin is covered!
> How blessed is the man to whom
> the LORD does not impute iniquity,
> And in whose spirit there is no deceit!
>   (Psalm 32:1-2)

David knew the blessing of forgiveness of sins. He knew the value of confessing his sin to God and the cleansing that comes from that confession, which was echoed by the apostle John: "If we confess our sins, He is faithful and righteous to forgive us our sins and to cleanse us from all unrighteousness" (1 John 1:9).

What about you? Do you know the forgiveness God gives when you call sin what it really is? Too often we excuse our behavior and rationalize what we think, say, and do. But God knows its sin, and He waits for us to realize this truth. When we confess sin to Him, there He is, ready to forgive and cleanse us from all unrighteousness.

If we anguish over our sin as David did in Psalm 32:3-4, we know that relief is just a confession away. Anguish doesn't have to last forever; it can be gone by morning. All we have to do is yield to the Holy Spirit's conviction and confess the sin, and then God forgives and cleanses us from that unrighteousness.

Sounds simple, doesn't it? It *is* simple! But it requires action. We must agree with God that we have sinned, and not just generally. We need to name specific sins before God—that's what confession is.

It's simple but very profound. The essence is agreeing with God's definitions and confessing them to Him—no excuse making, no quibbling, no arguing, just confession. God already knows sins. He simply wants us to see specific sins the way He does and confess them as failure to live according to His righteous standards. Sin is rebellion against these standards, twisting them to fit our disordered desires.

Your confession is simple, but it's difficult and sometimes even impossible for the arrogant. Oh, how we can drag the process out because we're too proud to admit our sin! We must have humility before God to confess sin. God resists the proud but gives grace to the humble. Confession of sin *is* humility, and God extends the grace of forgiveness and cleansing of unrighteousness to those who confess their sins.

What Is Your Desire?

ᔕᔕᔕᔕ

What does "He will give you the desires of your heart" (Psalm 37:4) mean? Does this depend on what your desires are? Yes it does, and God tells us in the psalms which desires are aligned with His Word. He's not about to give you your desire if that would ruin your life or someone else's!

Days One & Two

We're going to take two days to study Psalm 35 because of its length. First, read Psalm 35, marking the key words from your bookmark. Then go back through the psalm and underline or highlight the description of those who contend with David, the psalmist.

Now list David's attitude toward these people. Separately list what he asks God for. Now, looking at how David acts toward his enemies and how they act toward him, what do you see?

Read Matthew 5:43-48, a passage from the Sermon on the Mount, and the parallel passage in Luke 6:27-36. How do David's actions relate to Jesus' teaching about your enemies?

imprecatory — to invoke or call down curses upon someone

59

Think about your attitude toward your enemies. How do you measure up? Do you need to make any adjustments?

Other parts of the psalm seem to contradict this attitude of David's, but do they really? Or is he simply saying, "I leave it in your hands, Lord"? Cite the verses that support your answer.

Determine a theme for Psalm 35 and record it on PSALMS AT A GLANCE.

DAY THREE

Read Psalm 36 and mark the key words from your bookmark. Then list descriptions of God and the ungodly.

Now, what does David request of God for himself, for those who know God, and for the wicked? Think about how you relate to David's desires.

Finally, determine a theme for Psalm 36 and record it on PSALMS AT A GLANCE.

DAYS FOUR, FIVE, & SIX

Psalm 37 is so long we'll take three days to cover it. Read Psalm 37 and mark the key words and phrases from your bookmark. Also underline or highlight what David tells the reader to do and also the phrase *inherit the land* (or *earth*).

Now make lists of what you learn about each of these:

- what you should do

- what the people are like who will inherit the land

- what the wicked do and what will happen to them

∼ what the Lord is like and what He will do

∼ what the righteous are like and what is in store for them

How do the wicked and the righteous relate to God and to each other?

Do you see hints about when David wrote this psalm? Does his age help or hinder him to observe truth about the righteous, the wicked, and the Lord? Cite the verses that support your answers.

Record a theme for Psalm 37 on PSALMS AT A GLANCE.

DAY SEVEN

 Store in your heart: Psalm 36:5-7

Read and discuss: Psalms 35–37

QUESTIONS FOR DISCUSSION OR INDIVIDUAL STUDY

Psalm 35

∼ Discuss what David asks God to do about his enemies. What have they done that causes David to ask God for this help?

∼ How has David acted toward his enemies? How is this an example for us?

∼ What does David ask God to do for him? On what basis does David ask for vindication?

∼ What does David's cry to God teach us about taking things into our own hands instead of trusting God?

∾ What kind of justice does *God* give? How about *man?*

Psalm 36

∾ Discuss the contrast between the ungodly and those who take refuge in God.

∾ Discuss what you learned about God.

∾ Share your reactions to these truths about God and how they have helped you in your life.

Psalm 37

∾ Discuss the actions and fate of evildoers versus those who wait on the Lord. Whom does the Lord help and why?

∾ What are those who wait on the Lord to do? (Take your time; there's quite a list!)

∾ What does "delight yourself in the Lord" mean? What kinds of desires will the one who delights in the Lord have? What is the relationship between the desires of your heart and delighting in the Lord?

THOUGHT FOR THE WEEK

Delight yourself in the LORD;
And He will give you the desires of your heart.
  (Psalm 37:4)

Did you understand the last part of this verse? Did you understand the first part and the connection between the two? The desires of your heart are conditioned by your delight in the Lord. God will give you the desires that agree with your delight in Him.

Now, what does it mean to delight in the Lord? The next verse explains it well—commit your way to the Lord and trust Him. Delighting in the Lord means trusting Him and committing your way to Him.

But what do these mean? Proverbs 16 is an insightful cross-reference. The key is the heart—verse 1 says, "The plans of the heart belong to man." Verse 2 says, "All the ways of a man are clean in his own sight, but the LORD weighs the motives." In other words, we think we're doing fine; we rationalize what we plan (want) to do and then justify what we do. But the Lord weighs our motives. What we think and what the Lord thinks can be very different. We need to check our thoughts against what He thinks according to His Word.

We often fool ourselves into thinking we're operating out of a good motive when there's another bad one that really controls our actions. We convince ourselves we're doing the right thing with the right motive, but the truth is that something else is going on in our hearts and minds, sometimes motives we're not conscious of.

So what do we do? We apply 1 Chronicles 28:9, David's charge to his son Solomon:

> As for you, my son Solomon, know the God of your father, and serve Him with a whole heart and a willing mind; for the LORD searches all hearts, and understands every intent of the thoughts. If you seek Him, He will let you find Him; but if you forsake Him, He will reject you forever (1 Chronicles 28:9).

If we know the Lord understands every intent in every thought, we can ask Him to search our hearts. That's what David does in Psalm 139:23-24:

> Search me, O God, and know my heart;

> Try me and know my anxious thoughts;
> And see if there be any hurtful way in me,
> And lead me in the everlasting way.
>   (Psalm 139:23-24)

David knows that his own heart can deceive him, that he isn't the sure judge of his motives. He knows that God will measure our motives against His righteous standards. David knows that God's judgments will be holy, just, right, and true, and that He will expose motives that don't conform to His perfect standards.

Aligning our hearts with God's holy heart is the way we delight in the Lord. It's the only way we can commit our way to Him and really trust Him. This is an easy thing to say but a hard thing to do. It's a task we fail at often because we like to have control. Worse, we think we're in control and know how to do things. We partially trust our experience, training, talent, skill, intelligence, and the like. To wholly trust God is harder.

The starting point is David's cry in Psalm 139. Pray that God will reveal your motives and where you don't trust Him. Then yield to His will. When your desires are totally aligned with God's desires (His will), He will give you what you want—righteous desires from a righteous heart because you delight in Him.

James put it this way: "You ask and do not receive, because you ask with wrong motives, so that you may spend it on your pleasures." You might say, "I don't want to 'spend' on my pleasures; I want to 'spend' on God's work!" But if your heart is aligned with God, then your pleasure is God's pleasure. The key is having God search your heart to reveal those things not aligned with His will—even if they seem like they are.

Pray as David did. Ask God to reveal your motives. Then align your heart (motives) with His, and He'll give you the desires of your heart, which will be the desires of His heart.

WHAT PLEASES GOD?

∾∾∾∾

David wanted to please God and knew how to do it. Do you know what pleases God? This week's lesson will either confirm what you believe or surprise you because you were mistaken. Find out this week what pleases God.

∾∾∾
DAY ONE

Read Psalm 38 today, marking the key words from your bookmark.

In verses 1-10, what does David express? List the things he feels. How does he see himself? Why does he feel this way?

Have you ever felt this way? How do you feel about your sin? Are you normally aware of it?

According to verses 11-12, how do those around David see him? According to verse 13, how does David react to the way other people see him?

What does David ask for? Whom does he cry out to, and what does he want? Is this your heart's desire? In spite of what people say to or about you, do to you, or think about you, do you follow after righteousness? Do you trust God as David did?

Record a theme for Psalm 38 on PSALMS AT A GLANCE.

DAY TWO

Read Psalm 39, marking key words as usual.

What is the issue David deals with in verses 1-3? Read James 1:26 and 3:5-12. How are these verses related?

What does David ask for in verses 4-6? How does this idea relate to the one in verses 1-3?

Read Ecclesiastes 6:12; 3:12 and Isaiah 40:28. What is the contrast, and how does it help us understand our lives in God's plan? What does God promise those who believe the gospel? Does John 3:16 sound familiar?

What does David wait for according to verses 7-13? Read Isaiah 59:2 and compare this to what David cries for in verses 12-13. Does he hope for something in this life or in the next? Where should his hope be?

If you're in a situation like David's or feel the way he did in this psalm, how does 1 John 1:9 help you?

Record a theme for Psalm 39 on PSALMS AT A GLANCE.

DAY THREE

Read Psalm 40. Mark the key words from your bookmark. Now contrast this psalm with Psalm 39. What's the main difference?

List the praises David gives God in verses 1-5.

Read 1 Samuel 15:22-23. The narrative includes God telling Saul to utterly destroy the Amalekites—man, woman, child, and animal—and Saul sparing their king and the best of their flocks and herds. He claims he's doing this to sacrifice to God.

Compare this to Psalm 40:6-8. Is verse 8 true of you?

What characteristic does David declare about himself in verses 9-10? Read Acts 1:8 and 10:39-44. What is the value of a witness? How does it accomplish God's purposes?

Summarize David's confidence in God in verses 11-16. Do you have this confidence? Should you?

Record a theme for Psalm 40 on PSALMS AT A GLANCE.

DAY FOUR

Read Psalm 41, marking key words from your bookmark.

Summarize the main points made in each paragraph: verses 1-3, 4-9, 10-12, and 13.

What truths about God did you learn from this psalm? What does David expect God to do and why?

What did you learn about David's enemies?

Do you expect grace when you sin? On what basis? Read Romans 3:23-24.

Finally, record a theme for Psalm 41 on PSALMS AT A GLANCE.

DAY FIVE

Read Psalm 42 and mark the key words from your

bookmark. Also mark *soul* and *despair*[12] and add them to your bookmark.

The word *soul* is used only of living creatures. It characterizes the heart of man, his inner being. List what you learn about the soul from this psalm. The Hebrew word translated "despair" carries the sense of being low, bowing down, being humble.

What does the metaphor of a deer panting for water mean to you?

What is the antidote for despair?

Record a theme for Psalm 42 on PSALMS AT A GLANCE.

DAY SIX

Read Psalm 43 and mark the key words from your bookmark. Summarize the main ideas in verses 1-2, 3-4, and 5.

How does the psalmist describe his state in verse 2? But what does he know about God?

Read John 1:1-9; 8:12; and 14:6. How has God sent His light and truth?

Have you come to His holy hill and dwelling places?

Compare Psalm 43:5 with 42:11. Nothing indicates that the same psalmist wrote these verses, but the words convey the same sentiment. Do you see a connection between the two?

If you have come to God's holy hill by believing His light and truth, should your soul despair? How do we get out of despair once we're in it?

Finally, record a theme for Psalm 43 on PSALMS AT A GLANCE.

DAY SEVEN

 Store in your heart: Psalm 40:8
Read and discuss: Psalms 38–43

QUESTIONS FOR DISCUSSION OR INDIVIDUAL STUDY

ᴄᴠ For cach psalm this week, do the following:

- Summarize what you learn about God.

- Discuss the psalmist's feelings and situation.

- Discuss the truths about God that help the psalmist overcome despair.

ᴄᴠ When you come to Psalm 40, spend some time discussing the things God desires and how they can apply to your life. For example, what things today correspond to the sacrifices and offerings God *doesn't* want? What is more pleasing to Him?

ᴄᴠ When you discuss Psalm 42, compare your relationship to God with the psalmist's.

ᴄᴠ In your discussion of Psalm 43, include the impact of the light and truth in your life.

THOUGHT FOR THE WEEK

Saul had a problem. Though God chose him to be Israel's first king, he didn't understand the highest part of the calling. God wanted the king of Israel to represent His character to the people of Israel and the nations of the world.

Saul lived in the days of the tabernacle and the sacrificial system of worship God established at Mt. Sinai shortly after He rescued Israel from Egypt. He told His people He was holy, and He demanded that they be holy as well. He also ordained that each of Israel's future kings should make copies of the law before the Levitical priests, and that each king should read it all the days of his life. In this way he would learn to fear the Lord and carefully observe His law and statutes. (Read Deuteronomy 17:18-20 if you're not familiar with this requirement.)

The Bible doesn't record whether Saul made a copy of the law or even read it, but it does record times in his life when he did not fear the Lord and obey His commandments.

First Samuel 15 records God's directive to Saul to take vengeance on the Amalekites. The Amalekites had attacked stragglers at the rear of Israel at Rephidim as they marched wearily toward the land God promised them. The Amalekites had already rejected God, but this attack resulted in God's command to Saul to utterly destroy them. He intended this to show other nations what happens when a nation does not fear Him. God commanded Saul to kill men, women, children, infants, oxen, sheep, camels, and donkeys—all that Amalek had.

Saul partly obeyed and partly disobeyed. He captured Agag, king of the Amalekites, and the best of the sheep, oxen, fatlings, lambs, and all that was good, but he destroyed only what was despised and worthless.

God told Samuel what happened, and Samuel confronted Saul with his disobedience. Saul claimed he obeyed God, but bleating sheep and lowing oxen gave away his lie, so he next tried to justify his preserving the best animals for sacrifices to God. When pressed further he shifted the blame from himself to the people—that *they* wanted to sacrifice to God.

Samuel then confronted Saul with these words:

> Has the Lord as much delight in burnt
>   offerings and sacrifices

As in obeying the voice of the Lord?
Behold, to obey is better than sacrifice,
And to heed than the fat of rams.
For rebellion is as the sin of divination,
And insubordination is as iniquity and
idolatry.
(1 Samuel 15:22-23)

David knew this truth and even cited it in Psalm 40. On the surface, this seems contradictory. Didn't God set up the sacrificial system in the first place? He expected Israel to follow this system. But sacrifice is just a ritual—an outward performance that can be done without faith and other obedience. Many perform sacrifices and other rituals (like attending church) who do not fear and obey God. Ritual sacrifices ended when Rome destroyed Jerusalem's temple in AD 70. But even before that, Gentile Christians were not required to become Jews and follow the law's sacrificial system. The believer's inner heart and outward obedience mattered the most.

Those who truly fear God do His will because He has written His law on their hearts. This is possible only in the New Covenant with God, which we enter when we believe the gospel of Jesus Christ. Jeremiah and Ezekiel make it clear that this New Covenant changes hearts from stone to flesh, writes God's law on them, and puts the Holy Spirit (God Himself) in us to cause us to obey His statutes and commandments. Paul tells us clearly that all who believe the gospel of Jesus Christ are part of this New Covenant—all believers have this new heart with the law of God written on it, and all believers have the Holy Spirit indwelling to empower them to obey. When we disobey, we can't blame anyone but ourselves.

Do some believe sacrifice (ritual) is better than obedience today? Absolutely! Some go to church week after week, give a tithe of their incomes, study their Bibles, and pray, and yet they do not love their neighbors as themselves or as Christ loved them. They don't love their spouses as Christ loved the church. Is this obedience? Does this please God? Merely following the "rules" of the Christian life and looking good to others is easy enough. But Jesus told the scribes and Pharisees that while performing visible rituals, they neglected weightier matters of the law, such as justice, mercy, and faithfulness.

God expects us to obey not just ritually (externally) but from the heart—the essence of His two commandments. If we love God with all our heart, soul, mind, and strength, and love our neighbors as ourselves and as Christ loved us, we will please God. There is no room for shifting blame to others, no room for partial obedience. God wants *all* of us, all our love and obedience. Then He is pleased!

GREAT IS THE LORD

ᘓᘓᘓᘓ

"Great is the LORD, and greatly to be praised," says one psalm (96:4). "O clap your hands, all peoples," opens another (47:1). "God is our refuge and strength, a very present help in trouble" says a third (46:1). These familiar verses form a foundation for hope and confidence in the midst of life's troubles. Six psalms this week lay out different reasons for hope, all with a common goal—to bolster confidence in the Lord when life gets tough.

DAYS ONE & TWO

We'll take two days to cover Psalm 44 because of its length. Take your time reading and marking the key words on your bookmark.

Now, list the main point of each paragraph. Here are the NASB's paragraph divisions: verses 1-3, 4-8, 9-16, 17-19, and 20-26. If your Bible has different paragraphs, use them.

Now, what's the relationship between the first two paragraphs? Think about timing—do they refer to the past or future? Does one depend on the other? How does God act in both paragraphs?

What reaction does the psalmist have in verse 8? What principle do you see?

From verses 9-16, what's going on at the time of the psalmist's writing? In other words, what's the occasion for this psalm? Are the people mentioned doing something to themselves, or is God at work? How do you know?

How are the people reacting to their condition? Do they think they've caused this condition?

Finally, what does the psalmist ask God to do and on what basis?

Determine a theme for Psalm 44 and record it on PSALMS AT A GLANCE.

DAY THREE

Read Psalm 45 and mark the key words from your bookmark. Carefully watch for and mark all time references.

Who are the two main characters? Which verses address the first character? Which ones address the second character? List what you learn about the clothing of each character.

Read Psalm 45:14 and Matthew 25:1. What's happening in Matthew? In the psalm? What event do they both refer to? Read the psalm again with this in mind.

Many Old Testament prophecies speak of both present and future events. Let's see if Psalm 45 does this. List what you learn about the king in verses 3-5. Read Ephesians 5:25-32 and Revelation 19:7-19. From this and from the time phrases you've marked in Psalm 45, who is the king, and who is the bride?

Record a theme for Psalm 45 on PSALMS AT A GLANCE.

DAY FOUR

Today we'll cover two short psalms. First, read Psalm 46, marking the key words from your bookmark. Look for other repeated phrases that unlock the meaning. Mark them but don't add them to your bookmark.

What do you learn about God? What can you apply to your life?

Now read Psalm 47, marking key words and phrases from your bookmark plus other key words and phrases in this psalm.

Again, what did you learn about God? What is a proper response to God's nature and works?

Record themes for Psalms 46 and 47 on PSALMS AT A GLANCE.

DAY FIVE

Read Psalm 48, mark the key words, and then write down your observations about the city of God.

How do the kings of the earth react and why?

How do the people of God react to the city of God?

Record a theme for Psalm 48 on PSALMS AT A GLANCE.

DAY SIX

Psalm 49 is our last one for the week. According to our study pattern, observe it carefully, marking key words from your bookmark and others that are important in this psalm, like *wealth* or *riches*. You've marked *Redeemer* before; mark *redeem*[13] and *redemption*[14] the same way.

Who should listen to the psalmist? In the first paragraph, how does he describe his content?

Can one man redeem another by his wealth? Can wisdom save a man from dying? If no man can redeem his brother because the price for a soul is so high, who can?

What attitude should we have toward wealth and riches?

Well, that's it for this week, Beloved! Don't forget to record a theme for Psalm 49 on PSALMS AT A GLANCE.

DAY SEVEN

 Store in your heart: Psalm 48:1-2
Read and discuss: Psalms 44–49

QUESTIONS FOR DISCUSSION OR INDIVIDUAL STUDY

Psalm 44

- ∞ What principle did you learn about God's past works and our future? How does Psalm 44 illustrate this?

- ∞ When our lives are a mess and we think we've been forgotten by God, what should we do? What example does God give us using Israel in Psalm 44?

- ∞ On what basis can we have confidence in God?

Psalm 45

- ∞ Discuss prophetic implications of the bride and bridegroom in this psalm.

- ∞ What did you learn about God?

ꝏ Can you say what the psalmist does in verse 17? On what basis?

Psalms 46–48

ꝏ What common idea runs through these psalms?

ꝏ What praise choruses come to mind in the opening verses of each?

ꝏ Do you think these psalms are just for Israel or also for us?

ꝏ Discuss things you learned about God that you should praise Him for.

Psalm 49

ꝏ What attitude toward wealth and riches should we have?

ꝏ What does this psalm teach us about death?

ꝏ How do death, dying, and riches relate?

ꝏ Discuss who *can* and *can't* redeem you. Who redeems you? How do you know?

THOUGHT FOR THE WEEK

Let me ask you a question. Is the proverb "You can't take it with you" true? Do you understand it? Most often this is used to contrast the foolishness of amassing riches on earth with the wisdom of storing up treasures in heaven. And this is true! In the Sermon on the Mount, Jesus taught that where our treasures are, there our hearts will be also. His point is that we should be heavenly minded. We should seek God's kingdom first, believing that God will supply our needs—food, clothing, and shelter. Jesus did not mean that we shouldn't work for a living to provide these things. He did mean that we should understand that the ultimate source is God, not ourselves.

When we proudly say, "I earned that," we start down the path of self-sufficiency. We begin to buy into the lie that *we* are the ones who originate success (or status or wealth), not God. But every good and perfect thing we possess is a gift from God (James 1:17). Wealth is the product of God's grace.

"Oh," you say, "but the one who doesn't work much doesn't earn much." And you're right. Proverbs teaches us about the importance of diligent work and labor. "Go to the ant, O sluggard" (Proverbs 6:6), Solomon writes. In 2 Thessalonians, Paul says, "If anyone is not willing to work, then he is not to eat, either." Apparently at the time Paul wrote this letter, some Thessalonian people were sitting around doing nothing but waiting for the return of the Lord. Paul counseled them to labor until He comes.

Paul reminded his readers of his own example: working night and day, providing his own subsistence, not taking bread without paying for it, and not being a burden to others. He provided a prime example of a strong work ethic. But nowhere will you find Paul working to amass wealth or using riches to cause others to fear him. Psalm 49 says we have no reason to fear wealthy men. Many believe "their houses are forever," and so "they have called their lands after their own names." But ungodly houses and legacies don't endure. The wicked "are soon forgotten" (Ecclesiastes 8:10), and "their houses of ivory will also perish" (Amos 3:15). Their legacies are nothing.

In fact, one of this psalm's most important teachings about wealth is that death is the great equalizer. Wise or foolish, wealthy or poor, all die, and our wealth will not redeem us. Worldly wealth moves on to others, but it has no place in eternity.

The psalm proclaims another great truth: God redeems.

> No man can by any means redeem his brother
> Or give to God a ransom for him—
> For the redemption of his soul is costly,
> And he should cease trying forever—
> That he should live on eternally,
> That he should not undergo decay.
>   (Psalm 49:7-9)

God can't be bribed. The price He puts on a soul's redemption is beyond any man's ability to pay. God alone can and does redeem.

Do you see this? God redeems man on some basis other than man's attempted payments—whether money or labor ("works"). Regardless of what we do in this life, we can't pay the admission price to heaven. You can't buy or earn eternal life.

So what is the one way to eternal life for the poor and the rich, the wise and the fool? The answer is God's ransom. God Himself paid the price in His only begotten Son. The price God exacts for redemption is the shed blood of a man without sin. Paul's letter to the Romans teaches that all have sinned and fallen short of the glory of God and that no one is righteous. David penned the same truth, as we saw earlier (review Psalm 14:1-3). Romans also teaches us that the wages of sin is death. Everyone dies because everyone has sinned.

But every man lives on eternally. Man has a spirit component that endures beyond the body. And after resurrection, the whole man either suffers eternal punishment in the lake of fire (Revelation 20:14-15; Isaiah 66:24) or lives gloriously in heaven (Revelation 21–22). The difference between eternal death and eternal life is faith in the gospel of Jesus Christ (John 3:15-16).

Jesus, God's Son, gave Himself to redeem us (Titus 2:11-14). That was the costly redemption no one else could pay. So why fear man? His wealth may buy power and influence here on this earth, but it doesn't endure and can't save him. Sinful men can't buy redemption for themselves or for anyone else. Believe in God, believe in Jesus as your Redeemer, and you will live forever with Him in His kingdom.

How's Your Heart?

ᘱᘱᘱᘱ

Have you heard of the expressions *hard-hearted* or *heart of stone?* Today they are commonly used to describe someone who has no compassion. But the Scriptures teach that before any person believes the gospel, he has a heart of stone. And when he believes, God replaces that hard heart with a heart of flesh. How's your heart?

DAY ONE

Read Psalm 50, marking the key words from your bookmark as you have been doing. Having so many words on our bookmark may seem overwhelming, but I'll bet by now you're recognizing them in psalm after psalm without even looking at it.

What does God say to His people Israel in verses 1-15? What does He say to the wicked in verses 16-21? Do you see the contrast? How is this contrast summarized in verses 22-23?

If you have time today, make a list of all you learned about God from this psalm.

Record a theme for Psalm 50 on PSALMS AT A GLANCE.

DAY TWO

Psalm 51 almost certainly refers to David's adultery with Bathsheba. If you're not familiar with that story, read 2 Samuel 11–12:23. David commits adultery with Bathsheba, tries to cover up, and then orders his commander, Joab, to arrange for the death of Bathsheba's husband, Uriah.

With this background, let's read Psalm 51. Mark the key words on your bookmark. We mentioned earlier that the synonyms *sin, iniquity,* and *transgression* have a shade of difference in meaning in Hebrew. This psalm uses all three Hebrew words and highlights these slight differences.

The key here is not so much to understand these variations but to observe how David sees his sin once he recognizes it. You'll see true confession and repentance. Note what David asks God to do for him.

What does David say God wants rather than sacrifices?

Record a theme for Psalm 51 on PSALMS AT A GLANCE.

DAY THREE

We'll cover two short psalms today. Begin by reading Psalm 52 (just nine verses), marking the key words from your bookmark.

The setting of this psalm is 1 Samuel 21–22, when Saul was seeking to kill David. David had fled from Saul, and

Saul was pursuing David and his men. David went to Nob to Ahimelech the priest for help. One of Saul's men, Doeg the Edomite, was there and told Saul that David went to Ahimelech for help. Ahimelech rightly said he was not guilty of conspiring against Saul by helping David. But Saul rejected this and commanded his men to kill Ahimelech and all the priests at Nob. Saul's guards refused to kill God's priests, fearing the Lord. So Doeg the Edomite carried out the order.

This psalm is directed at Doeg and those like him. How does David describe him? What does David say God will do?

How does David contrast himself with this "mighty man"?

Record a theme for Psalm 52 on PSALMS AT A GLANCE.

Now read Psalm 53, marking key words and phrases from your bookmark. Also mark *fool.*

Read Psalms 10:4 and 14:1 and the context around these verses. What did you learn about those who think there is no God (atheists)?

Read Genesis 6:5 and Romans 3:10-12. What do these scriptures teach about depravity?

Verse 6 speaks of a time when God restores His captive people. But the Assyrian and Babylonian captivities are far in the future from David's time. What do you think verse 6 refers to and why?

Record a theme for Psalm 53 on PSALMS AT A GLANCE.

DAYS FOUR & FIVE

We'll cover two psalms over the next two days, one short

and one long. Let's tackle Psalm 54 first (just seven verses). Read Psalm 54, marking references to God. Underline every request David makes to God. Then highlight what David says he will do for God and why.

List truths about God's relationship to David. Are these true for you too?

Now read Psalm 55 and mark the key words on your bookmark. Don't miss synonyms for *prayer*, like *supplication, call,* and the like. Watch carefully for personal pronouns in verses 20-21. Read contexts before you mark them—ask if *he* and *his* refer to God or a man. (Note: If you are using the NIV or ESV, you won't have this problem. You'll see why when you read these verses.)

What problem does David come to God with? Whom is he asking God to help him with? What has this person done?

What does David ask God? How confident in God is he?

Would you do what David did in similar circumstances? Do you trust God as David did?

Finally, record themes for Psalms 54 and 55 on PSALMS AT A GLANCE.

DAY SIX

For our last day this week, read Psalm 56, marking the key words from your bookmark. Then note verses that are nearly identical.

Again, what is David's situation, and how does he handle it? How do David's actions indicate that he worships God?

What did you learn about God in this psalm that you can recite in difficult situations of life?

Record a theme for Psalm 56 on PSALMS AT A GLANCE.

DAY SEVEN

 Store in your heart: Psalm 51:10,17
Read and discuss: Psalms 51; 53

QUESTIONS FOR DISCUSSION OR INDIVIDUAL STUDY

- Discuss what you learned about God in these psalms.

- What did you learn about David—his sin and his attitude toward it?

- Discuss David's sins and how *sin, iniquity,* and *transgression* compare and contrast.

- Share insights about how your life is like David's.

- Share what these truths mean to you personally.

- What did you learn about life from these psalms? How will you apply these truths?

THOUGHT FOR THE WEEK

The story of David and Bathsheba is familiar to most people. Psalm 51 is David's response to God after Nathan confronts him with his sin. First John 1:9 tells us if we confess our sins, God is faithful and righteous to forgive and cleanse us from all unrighteousness. But first we need to recognize sin and call it that.

In this psalm David uses all three Hebrew words for sin, bringing out key ideas with each: *chatah* (failure to obey), *avon* (twisting or perverting God's standard), and *pasha* (rebellion). David *failed to obey* three of God's standards—don't covet your neighbor's wife, don't murder, and don't commit adultery.

David says he was brought forth (conceived) in iniquity, the fallen nature he inherited from Adam, which *twisted* God's standard. Adam and Eve ate from the forbidden fruit from the tree of the knowledge of good and evil in the garden of Eden (Genesis 3). Satan, the serpent, deceived Eve and led her to doubt God's goodness. Adam ate in spite of the fact that he was not deceived (1 Timothy 2:14).

David *rebelled* when he refused to go to war with his army, when he coveted his neighbor's wife, when he committed adultery with her, when he attempted to cover up by asking her husband to sleep with her, when he ordered Joab to send Uriah into the thick of a battle, and when he took Bathsheba to be his wife.

What does David conclude from these things in his psalms? He confesses that he was born in sin and committed sin. He declares that God desires truth in the inner being, where his sins originated. David shows that true confession includes admitting that his actions were sinful and agreeing with God's standards.

David also declares God's power to cleanse and even blot out sin, to create a new heart and spirit within, to revive, to restore joy. Repentant and forgiven sinners, David says, have a platform for testimony and evangelism. He is able to teach transgressors God's ways so sinners will be converted to God.

Stop and think about what you read in Psalm 51. Forgiven sinners can testify God's forgiveness to other sinners. While you're thinking you're worthless because of your sin, God says you're in perfect position to evangelize.

David didn't know the Messiah's name would be Jesus. He didn't tell people to believe in Jesus. What he did say was that sinners can testify to God's forgiveness, this will teach transgressors God's ways, and sinners will be converted (turned back) to God.

So you can testify too! The Great Commission in Matthew 28 is given to forgiven sinners. They are to declare the good news of forgiveness of sins through the atoning work of Jesus Christ, who—by becoming sin and paying the penalty for it by shedding His blood and rising from the dead—established everlasting life.

Jeremiah and Ezekiel prophesied the New Covenant Jesus inaugurated, declaring that God's people will have new hearts, hearts of flesh rather than the hearts of stone they're born with. They also prophesied that He will write His laws on their new hearts and put His Spirit in them to cause them to obey Him.

David asked God to give him a clean heart, a steadfast spirit, and a permanent indwelling of His Holy Spirit. Jeremiah and Ezekiel had not been born when David wrote this, yet David knew that God had the power to do these things and that they were necessary if he was to worship God and serve Him by testifying to His forgiveness.

TAKING REFUGE IN GOD

ᕔᕔᕔᕔ

Saul envied David's popularity and wanted to kill him. But David knew that Saul was God's anointed, so David didn't defend himself or raise a hand against Saul. Instead he sought refuge in a cave in the wilderness. The cave was a physical refuge, but David was really taking refuge in God. What about you? How do you take refuge when you're persecuted?

ᕔᕔᕔ

DAY ONE

Read Psalm 57. Mark the key words on your bookmark. Mark *refuge*[15] and add it to your bookmark.

List what you learned about God and about David's relationship to God. Then consider your relationship to God. Do you see Him the way David did? Do you take refuge in Him the way David did?

Determine a theme for Psalm 57 and record it on PSALMS AT A GLANCE.

DAY TWO

Read Psalm 58, marking key words as before.

Now list what you learned about the righteous and unrighteous and about God's judgment. How do you fit into God's judgment?

Determine a theme for Psalm 58 and record it on PSALMS AT A GLANCE.

DAY THREE

Psalm 59 is also set in the context of Saul trying to capture or kill David. Follow our usual pattern today, reading Psalm 59 and marking key words.

What are David's enemies like? What is God like? What does David ask God to do for him? What does David know about God? Remember, *lovingkindness*[16] is a covenant term.

Do you know God the way David did?

Determine a theme for Psalm 59 and record it on PSALMS AT A GLANCE.

DAY FOUR

Joab was David's general of the Israelite army. Read 2 Samuel 8:16. Some manuscripts read "Edom" here, and Psalm 60 may be referring to this passage. Read Psalm 60, marking the key words from your bookmark.

What is the situation? How does David see God? What does David know about God and what He will do? What about you—what do you know about God?

Determine a theme for Psalm 60 and record it on PSALMS AT A GLANCE.

DAY FIVE

Read Psalm 61 and mark the key words from your bookmark.

No specific Bible event is associated with this psalm, but it fits the ideas of the psalms around it. List what you learned about God, about what He did for David and what He will do. Then note what David promises to do. How much like David are you?

Determine a theme for Psalm 61 and record it on PSALMS AT A GLANCE.

DAY SIX

Read through Psalm 62, marking key words. As with Psalm 61, no specific biblical event is mentioned, so the theme is David's general reliance on God.

List what you learned about God, David's enemies, and David. Then reflect on David's relationship to God and your own.

Record a theme for Psalm 62 on PSALMS AT A GLANCE.

DAY SEVEN

 Store in your heart: Psalm 57:5

Read and discuss: Psalms 57–62

QUESTIONS FOR DISCUSSION OR INDIVIDUAL STUDY

- ∾ Discuss your insights on God from Psalms 57–62.

- ∾ What did you learn about David and his relationship with God from these psalms?

- ∾ How do these things apply to your daily life?

- ∾ How does your prayer life compare to David's?

- ∾ How does your worship compare to David's? What are the similarities and differences?

THOUGHT FOR THE WEEK

When a storm comes, we take refuge. In parts of the U.S. where tornados are common, people take shelter in cellars. Baby animals seek the shelter of their mothers. Birds provide shelter to their young with their wings.

David was more popular than Saul after killing the giant Goliath and commanding Saul's army to victory elsewhere. The people sang songs extolling David's superior campaigns to Saul's, and Saul became naturally envious. Eventually he sought to kill David.

We might not try to kill people, but we can certainly sympathize with coveting others' wealth and status. We can easily be driven to seek what they have. And we can build up a case for why we don't like them. Then we can create plans to surpass them.

Most people are content trying to do better than others, but others try to get rid of their competitors. This was the case when figure skater Tonya Harding tried to have her rival Nancy Kerrigan's knees broken. Envy drove Tonya to angry, desperate measures.

Most of us won't take these measures, but we sometimes

think hurtful thoughts. When we do, we buy into the lies of the enemy, thinking his thoughts. We should rather focus on whatever is lovely, pure, honorable, and true, as Paul wrote (Philippians 4:8).

Instead of trying to beat or eliminate the competitors we're envious of, we should trust God. We should take refuge in Him, in the shelter of His wings, and let Him solve what we see as the problem. Taking refuge in God means trusting Him in all circumstances. And when we trust Him, we worship Him.

Too often we think of worship as music and lifting our hands, that is, a set of rituals. We relegate these rituals to a set day and time of the week. These and other rituals can be proper elements of a worship service, but true worship is not restricted to these external actions and certain days and times of the week. Worship includes belief, attitude, and lifestyle. How we live our lives is important; in fact, if we live consistently according to God's Word, our entire life is worship.

David understood this. He expressed worship to God in these psalms by declaring God's character, salvation, and faithfulness. David knew that it wasn't his job to take care of his enemies, it was God's. And he showed this by not lifting his hand against the Lord's anointed king. We too can show this by not lifting up our hands against our enemies.

Vengeance is the Lord's—He alone is a just judge. Only He is 100 percent right in deciding consequences for actions. He never designs a consequence that is too light or too extreme. He never acts late or early, and He never makes a mistake.

By contrast, we rarely do things quite right. We certainly are not able to in our flesh. We follow God's Word but never perfectly. We live in a body of flesh that wars against the spirit. We do things that aren't Christlike, that don't reflect God's perfection.

But we can trust God because He judges perfectly. When we take refuge in Him, we are free of concern for justice on our enemies. We know each person will receive perfect justice in perfect time.

This is easier said than done. Our flesh rises up. We listen to the lies of the enemy, the father of lies, the great deceiver, the adversary of our souls and accuser of the brethren. He always tells us and God we're wrong. But we have an advocate with the Father, His Son, the Lord Jesus Christ, who paid the price for our sin. The Father knows this. So we shouldn't listen to Satan, the accusing liar; we should listen to and obey the God of truth and redemption.

We must guard against the schemes of the devil. We must put on spiritual armor to fight a spiritual battle. We must trust the Lord at all times.

Take refuge in Him. Ask Him to deliver you at all times.

LOVINGKINDNESS
IS BETTER THAN LIFE

What do we treasure the most? Life? Certainly we value life and treat it as precious. We try to save lives and prevent deaths by spending billions on safety and health. But the psalmist says God's lovingkindness is better than life (63:3). What did he mean? How could he say that? You'll find out this week.

DAY ONE

Read Psalm 63 and mark the key words from your bookmark. Again, record your insights about God and David's relationship to Him.

What pattern of worship do you see in this psalm? What is David's motivation to praise God? How often and in what circumstances should you praise Him?

You might recognize the praise chorus from verses 3 and 4. Take a moment to sing it aloud.

Now read Psalm 64, following the same instructions. Did you notice the change of environment? What is David's situation now? What do his enemies do? What does David trust

God to do, and what is the result of God's actions? How does this psalm describe worship of God?

Be sure to record themes for these psalms on PSALMS AT A GLANCE.

DAY TWO

Read Psalm 65 and mark the key words from your bookmark. Then list what you learned about God.

In this psalm, what is man's response to truths about God? How does creation respond? How do you respond?

Record a theme for this psalm on PSALMS AT A GLANCE.

DAYS THREE & FOUR

Studying two psalms is our goal for these two days. One is very short. Start by reading Psalm 66 and marking the key words from your bookmark. I'll bet you've got them memorized by now!

Now, what is the main idea of this psalm? What truths about God do you see? Israel would immediately recognize references to the crossing of the Red Sea and Joshua's conquering the land of Canaan. Did you see them? These are things Israel could praise God for. How can these truths about what God has done motivate you to praise Him? What has He done for you that you can praise Him for?

What did you learn about prayer in Psalm 66?

Now read Psalm 67, a mere 7 verses but powerful ones. Mark key words as usual. Why does the psalmist ask for God's grace and blessing? Who is mentioned a lot in this psalm? Who receives salvation? Who praises God?

Now record themes for these two psalms on PSALMS AT A GLANCE.

DAYS FIVE & SIX

Psalm 68 is a bit longer than this week's other psalms, so we'll take two days to explore its message to us about worship. Begin by reading it and marking the key words from your bookmark. Take your time and soak in the message.

As usual, God is the central figure. Ask the 5 W's and an H questions about Him and list what you learn about His nature and works—both things to praise Him for.

Record a theme for Psalm 68 on PSALMS AT A GLANCE.

DAY SEVEN

 Store in your heart: Psalm 63:3-4

Read and discuss: Psalms 63; 65–68

QUESTIONS FOR DISCUSSION OR INDIVIDUAL STUDY

- ∾ Discuss your insights about praising God.

- ∾ What attributes of God are you most thankful for?

- ∾ How do you praise God? In what ways? When? Why?

∞ What is the relationship between sin, forgiveness, and praise to God?

∞ Discuss the relationship of "the nations" to God. What should they do and why?

∞ What is the relationship between the earth and God?

∞ What does it mean for God to bear our burdens?

THOUGHT FOR THE WEEK

Thy lovingkindness is better than life,
Thy lovingkindness is better than life.
My lips shall praise Thee, thus I will bless Thee.
I will lift up my hands unto Thy name.*

I learned this praise chorus early in my Christian life. Look at the words carefully. They come from the King James Version of Psalm 63:3-4. These two verses express powerful truths for our lives that are echoed throughout the psalms.

First, we recognize that God's lovingkindness is better than life. This truth captures several ideas. *Lovingkindness* is a covenant term. It expresses a faithful, constant love that depends only on God's faithfulness, not our worth, performance, attractiveness, talents, skills, education…any of the things the world values and measures. It is available to those who have believed the gospel of Jesus Christ—that Jesus who was sinless from conception took our sins, willingly offering Himself as a substitutionary sacrifice for us. Because the wages of sin is death, Jesus died to bear our sins. "The Lord, who daily bears our burden," Psalm 68:19 says, "the God who is our salvation." God bears our everyday burdens out of

---

* Hugh Mitchell, "Thy Loving Kindness," © 1956 Singspiration Music. All rights reserved. Used by permission.

lovingkindness, and He bore our burden of sin once for all: "For God so loved the world that He gave His only begotten Son, that whosoever believes in Him shall not perish, but have eternal life" (John 3:16). We enter into the New Covenant with God through faith, and His covenant lovingkindness extends to us forever.

Another thing we learn from these two little verses is that this lovingkindness is better than anything in this life. "Whoa!" you say, "What about my children, my spouse, my parents? I love them!" Some people love their possessions, their professions, their status. But nothing in this life is better than God's lovingkindness. Do you remember the call to discipleship Jesus gave in Luke to "hate" father, mother, spouse, children, and even our own life? God's lovingkindness is better than all these relations and even our own lives. David knew this. He lost a child to death because of his sin with Bathsheba, but he still clung to God. He knew his relationship to God was the most important thing he had.

We also learn that we bless God when we praise Him with our lips and hands. Some teach that we can't bless God; God alone can bless. It's true that He blesses us, but according to Scripture we also bless Him with praise. Generally God blesses us with power for salvation, success, prosperity, health, and the like. We can't bless God this way. But throughout Scripture we read of blessings toward God. The idea is the opposite of curses—we speak well of Him, not ill. We extol His virtues; we praise Him and don't accuse Him. We declare His goodness to Him even though He already knows it. This is humility, and some think the Hebrew word translated "bless" is related to kneeling, one of the signs of humility. Blessing God shows our humility in acknowledging Him as the source of all we have.

In addition to kneeling with folded hands and bowed

heads, we learn from Scripture that lifting up hands to God is another humble approach to Him. Solomon prayed this way at the dedication of the temple, and Paul commanded men everywhere to pray, lifting up holy hands (1 Timothy 2:8).

Lifting up empty hands is significant, showing that what you have comes from God. It equally shows that God can take what you have anytime because it's His possession, on loan to you. Empty hands show willingness to receive what God gives, but our hands need to be holy, pure, clean—not "covered with blood" (see Isaiah 1:15). Who may ascend to the hill of God and stand in His holy place? Psalm 24 asks. The answer is this: the one with clean hands and a pure heart.

WHEN MY HEART WAS EMBITTERED

∿∿∿∿

David said, "Until I came into the sanctuary of God... my heart was embittered and I was pierced within...I was senseless and ignorant; I was like a beast before You" (Psalm 73:17,21-22). How much like senseless beasts we are when we're bitter. How senseless and ignorant it is to envy those who possess nothing more than this world's status and wealth. We need God to open our eyes so we can see differently.

∿∿∿

DAYS ONE & TWO

Psalm 69 is long enough to take two days. We always want to approach our study with sufficient time to look at what the text says, understand what it means, and reflect on its application. So let's not hurry through our study as if it were an item to check off our to-do list. Read the psalm slowly and carefully, marking the key words from your bookmark. Also mark *reproach*[17] and add it to your bookmark. Remember, marking helps you slow down to focus on what's important in the text.

Now, how does David start this psalm in the first four verses? Do you feel the way he does sometimes? Look at verses 5-12. Describe the change in David. Also, contrast his motivation with the way he was treated.

Notice the "but" at the start of verse 13. What does this tell you? Compare verses 2-3 with verse 14, and then make a list of what David does and asks.

Now follow this pattern throughout the rest of the psalm.

Now that you've done all this work, read the psalm again and look for references that remind you of Jesus. Psalms often have a prophetic feature. If you need help getting started, compare verse 21 with Matthew 27:34.

Determine a theme for this psalm and record it on PSALMS AT A GLANCE.

DAYS THREE & FOUR

We have two psalms to cover in the next two days, one very short and one a bit longer. Start by reading Psalm 70, marking the key words from your bookmark. It should be easy to see what the main idea is in this five-verse psalm of David. List what David asks God to do and what he says those who seek God should do.

Then record the theme on PSALMS AT A GLANCE.

Now turn to Psalm 71. This psalm contains many familiar ideas, so it's sort of a review. But read it, marking key words as you have done before, and don't hurry. Remember to mark references to time—they're very important in this psalm.

There's no superscription to tell us the setting, but there are clues that tell us when the psalmist composed this psalm. That's one reason to always look for and mark references to time. The cry of his heart is based on his age. Perhaps you can relate now. If not, later you will.

What does the psalmist say God has done for him, and what does he plan to do for God? (Make two lists.)

Finally, record a theme for Psalm 71 on PSALMS AT A GLANCE.

DAY FIVE

Solomon, David's son and royal heir by Bathsheba, composed Psalm 72. As you read and mark key words today, mark *king* but don't add it to your bookmark.

Some facts about Solomon will help you understand this psalm. Read 1 Kings 3:6-28; 9:26–10:29 for background.

Now list what Solomon asks for. Note how Solomon ends this psalm in verses 18-19. Think about this: Did Solomon ask these things for his glory or God's?

Record a theme for Psalm 72 on PSALMS AT A GLANCE.

By the way, Psalms is divided into five books, and we've now finished two! We're almost halfway through!

DAY SIX

Read Psalm 73 today, marking key words as usual.

You may notice in book 3 of Psalms that many are attributed to Asaph. We're not sure who this person was, but a Levite musician during David's reign had this name, and so did a recorder in the days of Hezekiah. What we *are* certain of is that these psalms are the Word of God, praises to Him in worship, truth to comfort and sustain us in our lives.

What issue causes Asaph to write this psalm?

List what you learned about the wicked. Have you ever felt the way Asaph did toward the wicked?

What changed Asaph's heart? Has the same thing happened to you? Are you now like the Asaph described in verses 23-28?

Spend some time worshipping God for what He planned and did for you, Beloved. Kneel before Him, pray a prayer of thanksgiving, and praise Him.

Record a theme for Psalm 73 on PSALMS AT A GLANCE.

DAY SEVEN

 Store in your heart: Psalm 73:26

Read and discuss: Psalms 69–73

QUESTIONS FOR DISCUSSION OR INDIVIDUAL STUDY

- Have the group get out their PSALMS AT A GLANCE Chart and discuss the main themes of the five psalms in this week's study. What issues are addressed? How are they similar? How are they different?

- Spend some time talking about the prophecies about Jesus in Psalm 69.

- Discuss aging according to Psalm 71. How does this compare with the world's attitude today?

- Discuss the relevance of Psalm 72 to today's leaders. Contrast self-promotion with giving God glory.

- Discuss what you learned about envy and bitterness

from Psalm 73. How does God set us straight when we're trapped in these sins? What did you learn about truth?

∽ What struck you most deeply in these psalms?

THOUGHT FOR THE WEEK

Asaph the psalmist bares his soul to God in Psalm 73. There he shows how he suffered from envying the arrogant as he looked at their lives. They seemed without pain, fat with riches, not in trouble, having none of the ordinary plagues other men had. They seemed to get along without God, even speculating that He didn't know what they were doing.

When Asaph looked at their long, rich, and easy lives, he grew envious. He saw his attempts to be pure as vain. The suffering he endured so he could live a righteous life seemed worthless compared to the prosperity of wicked people.

The same temptation reaches us. But 1 Corinthians 10:13 promises that these temptations are common to us all and are not beyond God's help. He does not allow us to be tempted beyond what we are able. He provides a way of escape so we can endure:

> No temptation has overtaken you but such as is common to man; and God is faithful, who will not allow you to be tempted beyond what you are able, but with the temptation will provide the way of escape also, so that you will be able to endure it.

Temptation to envy is common, but we can bear it because God helps us. That's what Asaph understood. He saw the life of ease, compared it to his own difficult life, and got bitter. But God helped him out of this mire because he entered the sanctuary of God.

I don't think Asaph meant the temple when he referred to "the sanctuary of God." I think he meant coming to understand God's Word. God gave him an understanding of the end of wicked men. He clearly saw their end in contrast to his own. They and their wealth would be destroyed.

Believers are aliens and strangers on earth, citizens of heaven. You and I and all who believe have an eternal perspective through which we view the temporal issues of life. Asaph had that too but became ensnared by envy, which led to bitterness. Then God snapped him out of it!

Such things can happen to Christians today. The New Testament describes envy as one of those bad traits we had before our new birth—a past way of thinking (1 Corinthians 6:10-11). A residual carries forward in the flesh according to Galatians 5:17, and according to the context, it wars against the Spirit. The Spirit and the new spirit in the believer win this war, but those who *practice* the things of the flesh their entire lives do not inherit the kingdom of God.

The rest of Galatians 5 tells us to exhibit the fruit of the Spirit because we have crucified the flesh. We have power through the indwelling Holy Spirit to conquer the draw of the flesh. But sometimes we still sin these sins.

Peter gives us a solution in 1 Peter 2:1. We are to put aside envy and other inner sins and long for the pure milk of the Word, which will help us mature spiritually. The Word of God teaches us what's wrong and what's right. Additionally, the Word itself works in us with supernatural power. It judges the thoughts and intentions of the heart, as Hebrews 4:12 tells us.

When we study God's Word, we step into His sanctuary. There He meets us with pure truth that sets us free from fleshly snares. Oh, we'll still encounter those snares, but if we know God's Word, we can spot and avoid them. But even if we're snared, God's Word provides the way of escape so we can praise Him for what He has done for us and worship Him for what He will do for us.

I REMEMBER

As we age, sometimes we reflect on our lives, remembering things that have influenced us. Some memories are fond, some are not. The psalmist remembers the deeds of the Lord and encourages us to remember them too. They contain lessons for life—eternal life.

DAY ONE

Read Psalm 74, marking key words from your bookmark. Also mark *remember* and add it to your bookmark. You'll see this word in several psalms this week.

Make a list of what you learned about God.

Now, what issue provokes this psalm? What's going on? What does the psalmist ask God to do? Why? What did you learn about God that might explain why the psalmist asks Him to act?

Have you ever felt the way the psalmist felt about God's reputation?

Record a theme for Psalm 74 on PSALMS AT A GLANCE.

DAY TWO

Today is another two-psalm day. Start by reading Psalm 75, marking key words and time indicators.

List what you learned about God. What does the psalmist say he will do?

Now read Psalm 76 and mark the key words from your bookmark. Salem (verse 2) is Jerusalem, which is also often referred to as Zion. Mount Zion is one of the hills in Jerusalem.

What did you learn about God? According to this psalm, what is the purpose of God's judgment?

Record themes for Psalms 75 and 76 on PSALMS AT A GLANCE.

DAY THREE

Read Psalm 77 today and mark the key words from your bookmark.

Note the psalmist's situation. What is he doing? How does he feel? What are his questions about God?

What does the psalmist vow to remember? What should you and I remember about God?

Record a theme for Psalm 77 on PSALMS AT A GLANCE.

DAYS FOUR, FIVE, & SIX

Psalm 78 is long so we'll take three days to cover it. Don't panic! We'll take it one bite at a time. Spread your study over three days; take your time. Start by reading through the psalm, marking key words. Then we'll dig in one paragraph at a time. List in your notebook what you learn.

What pattern do you see for parents in verses 1-8?

What negative example do you find from the sons of Ephraim? What did you learn about God in verses 9-20 that should have kept the sons of Ephraim from disobeying?

Was the Lord justified to act (verses 21-22)? The events described are from the wilderness wanderings during the Exodus and are recorded in Numbers and Deuteronomy. What do you learn about God from His actions in verses 23-31?

What actions of God brought Israel back to Him? Did they come wholeheartedly? Again, what did God's response to Israel's disobedience teach you about His character? The events in verses 43-53 occurred in Egypt and are found in Exodus. Verses 54-64 are recounted in Judges and 1 Samuel. Once more, what did you learn about God? Was He justified when He acted? What is God's motivation for these acts?

How does the psalm end (verses 65-72)? Why does it end this way? What does this tell you about when the psalm was written? (If you are unfamiliar with Israel's history, just skip this question.)

Finally, record a theme for Psalm 78 on PSALMS AT A GLANCE.

DAY SEVEN

 Store in your heart: Psalm 77:13

Read and discuss: Psalms 74–77 or Psalm 78. (You probably won't have time to discuss all the psalms.)

QUESTIONS FOR DISCUSSION OR INDIVIDUAL STUDY

For Psalms 74–77

∽ Discuss how you would feel if you thought God had rejected you forever. Can you identify with the psalmist's frustration?

∽ Discuss truths about God in Psalm 74:12-17. Why are these things important?

∽ Why does the psalmist ask God to remember things and urge Him to action?

∽ Discuss what you learned about judgment in Psalms 75 and 76. How is this comforting?

∽ What truths about God from these two psalms give you comfort and confidence?

∽ Ask the group to share a time when their prayers to God seemed similar to the psalmist's in Psalm 77:1-4.

∽ What does the psalmist hold on to, and how does his example instruct and encourage you?

∽ What did you learn from these psalms that will impact your life? What truths will affect your relationship with God? What lessons will you commit to live out?

For Psalm 78

∽ Discuss events of the Exodus that testify to God's power.

∽ Discuss Israel's disobedience against God's faithfulness and patience.

∽ How does knowing God's patience and faithfulness help you?

∽ Discuss how you relate to the Israelites, who sinned even though they knew about God's mighty wonders.

∽ What is the New Testament parallel to David's shepherding Israel? How does Jesus shepherd you?

∽ What have you learned from this study that will impact your life? What truths will affect your relationship with God? What lessons will you commit to live out?

THOUGHT FOR THE WEEK

Memory is a funny thing. What we remember changes over time. What really happened doesn't change, but what we remember changes. As we age, our short-term memory begins to fail; we can't recall a multitude of things like where we left our keys, someone's name, dates, details of what doctors told us to do. But our long-term memory improves. My grandfather told me stories from his boyhood that I'd never heard. His long-term memory recalled events that really happened but had remained locked for years. He told me those stories, and I passed them down to the next generation so they wouldn't be forgotten. But there are many things from his past that he never told me. If only he had written them down.

In thinking about these issues, I realize that where I leave my keys is relatively unimportant. Short-term memory loss is not usually as significant as it is annoying and frustrating. But long-term memories can be valuable, not to the world perhaps, but to my family.

We saw something like this in this week's psalms. Long-term memory of Israel's victorious exodus from Egypt and acquisition of the promised land was crucial. These deeds of the Lord were critical to Israel's understanding of who God is and what He is like. If they were forgotten, only immediate circumstances would matter to Israel, and these could be crushing. For example, when they were captive in Babylon and the temple in Jerusalem was destroyed, if all they had was short-term memory, they would see God as unfaithful, vindictive, destructive, and unloving.

That's why Moses started the process of recording history in what we call the Scriptures. God used Moses to record what needed to be known for all time. It needed to be written so that it was free from the vagaries of memory. Because memory would fail, without copies of the law (the Torah), Israel would not know how God rescued them from captivity in Egypt. They would not know God's plagues on the Egyptians, His parting of the Red Sea, His destruction of Pharaoh's army, His leading them through the wilderness, and His conquering the land promised to Abraham, Isaac, and Jacob.

Until oral tradition was captured in Scripture, generations had to pass these stories along verbally, or the next generation would never know them. The national memory needed to be long-term to appreciate the faithful lovingkindness of God. And so God provided the Scriptures. Now, if only people would read the Scriptures, they would know the things that happened a long time ago, things God did that give His people the confidence and hope that God intended in His holy Word.

Although in literate cultures we have the ability to read and ready access to inexpensive reading materials, we don't read as much as we should. The majority of recent high school graduates in the U.S. today say they'll never voluntarily read another book ever again. And this spells disaster for the church. Bible reading and study continues to decline, and so the church doesn't remember what God has done and taught. If we neglect God's Word, we will be doomed to repeat avoidable situations and doomed to live through consequences we could have prevented.

The days of Israel's judges were like this. Israel lived by short-term memory, forgetting what the Scripture told them, not recalling the recent deliverance by God from the trouble they had at the hands of an oppressor. They played the harlot with foreign gods, so God sent a new oppressor so they would turn to Him. When Israel cried out to God, He sent a deliverer, and Israel had peace. And then Israel repeated the cycle again and again.

In Deuteronomy, God told Israel to teach His commandments diligently to their sons and talk of them when they were sitting in their houses and when they were walking by the way, when they lay down and when they rose up. They were to bind them as a sign on their hands, their foreheads, and their doorposts and gates. Israel obeyed literally with phylacteries and mezuzahs, but they failed with respect to really knowing God's Word.

How do we know? Just read the history of Israel. In fact, during Josiah's reign in Judah, the book of the law had been lost in the house of the Lord and was only discovered when workers were cleaning out and restoring the temple. The parallel for us today is that so few people in the church read and understand the Bible. Our challenge is to continue telling the stories, to continue passing down to the next generation the things that God has done so that they know God's character and ways.

LISTEN TO ME

As a little girl was telling her daddy a story, he kept saying "Uh-huh," but he was distracted by what he was doing. She knew he wasn't interested, so she said, "Daddy, listen to me *with your eyes.*" She knew that if he stopped and looked at her, she would have his attention, and he would hear what she was saying. God says the same thing to us: *Listen to Me with the eyes of your heart* (see Ephesians 1:18).

DAY ONE

Read Psalm 79 today, marking key words from your bookmark as you have been doing.

What was the situation in Israel or Judah when this psalm was written? What is the psalmist's complaint and request? On what basis does he ask?

Make a list of what you learned about God.

Read Psalm 74 again. Compare and contrast it with Psalm 79.

Record a theme for Psalm 79 on PSALMS AT A GLANCE.

DAY TWO

Read Psalm 80, marking key words as usual. Look for time indicators.

What or who does the vine represent? Is the situation in Psalm 80 like the one in Psalm 79? What method does the psalmist use in Psalm 80 to cry out to God?

What did you learn about God? The names of God are important—each one reflects an aspect of God. "God of hosts"[18] is a translation of the Hebrew words *Elohim Sabaoth,* which we find also in Romans and James. God has hosts, an army that can avenge His people and deal with the nations.

Record a theme for Psalm 80 on PSALMS AT A GLANCE.

DAY THREE

Read Psalm 81 today and mark the key words from your bookmark. How has the tone changed from the previous psalm?

Note the psalmist's situation. Is Israel in the same condition as in the previous psalm?

What did you learn about God? How does He answer questions raised in Psalm 80 in this psalm? Does this message speak to you today?

Record a theme for Psalm 81 on PSALMS AT A GLANCE.

DAY FOUR

This is another two-psalm day. Start by reading Psalm 82, marking the key words from your bookmark.

Now, what's the simple message in this short psalm? Record a theme for Psalm 82 on PSALMS AT A GLANCE.

Now read Psalm 83, repeating our usual method of marking key words from your bookmark.

What is the situation in Israel according to this psalm? How is it different from that in Psalms 74 and 80? What's the common idea? What does Asaph call on God to do?

If you don't know the stories referred to in verses 9-12, read Judges 7–8.

More names of God appear in verse 18. The text says God's name is the LORD (Yahweh or Jehovah) and that He is "Most High," a translation of *Elyon*. The nations have their gods, but Israel's God, Jehovah, is the Most High. He is *the* God.

Now record a theme for Psalm 83 on PSALMS AT A GLANCE.

DAY FIVE

Two more psalms today. Start by reading Psalm 84 and marking the key words from your bookmark.

The temple (house of the Lord) is prominent in this psalm. What is the main idea about the courts or house of God?

Now read Psalm 85 and mark the key words from your bookmark.

The setting of this psalm by the sons of Korah is hard

to determine. It occurs after God has done something for Israel—what? What does the psalmist ask God to do?

What did you learn about God in this psalm? What did you learn about the psalmist? Is he listening to God?

Record themes for Psalms 84 and 85 on PSALMS AT A GLANCE.

DAY SIX

Our final psalm for this week is 86, another psalm of David. Notice that the superscription says it is a prayer of David. When you can't find words to pray yourself, consider reading this psalm.

Now read and mark as you have done before.

How does David describe himself? How does he describe God? What does David ask God to do, and what does David promise to do?

Finally, record a theme for Psalm 86 on PSALMS AT A GLANCE.

DAY SEVEN

 Store in your heart: Psalm 84:10

Read and discuss: Psalms 79–86

QUESTIONS FOR DISCUSSION OR INDIVIDUAL STUDY

∾ What characteristics of God do the psalmists (Asaph, the sons of Korah, and David) cling to in these psalms? What about you? Do you cling to them too?

∾ The psalmists cry out to God to save or call Him the God of their salvation. What does *salvation* mean in the context of these psalms?

∾ Discuss the names of God used in these psalms and their implications for your life.

∾ In Psalm 83, the psalmist asked God not to remain quiet. Describe how you listen when God speaks. Or does He speak today? If so, how?

∾ Israel had a physical tabernacle and then a temple to go to. But what did the psalmist mean about one day in God's courts being better than a thousand outside? What application can you make for your life?

THOUGHT FOR THE WEEK

The psalmist cried out to God to speak. Perhaps God seemed to him to be silent, for he hadn't heard God speak. But maybe God was speaking, and he just wasn't listening or didn't hear. Maybe he needed to listen with his eyes.

God speaks to us in many ways. Some people love to quote 1 Kings 19:12, in which God speaks to Elijah on Mt. Sinai in a "still small voice." This is the King James Version translation—others translate it as a gentle blowing or a low whisper. And from that they say, "God speaks in a still small voice." And He did then. But God speaks in other ways too.

Certainly at Mt. Sinai in Exodus 19, when Moses spoke, God answered him with thunder. In chapter 20, Israel acknowledged that God was speaking in the thunder and lightning and trumpets, and they asked Moses to speak to them, for they were terrified and sure they would die.

The Scripture recounts how God called to Abraham, to

Jacob, and then to Moses from the burning bush. He called to the young boy Samuel, who while serving Eli at the tabernacle heard God calling his name audibly and thought it was Eli. God spoke audibly to Jesus at His baptism, to Paul on the road to Damascus, and to Ananias in Damascus. He spoke at the transfiguration and in Jerusalem (John 12:28). So we know God has spoken audibly, and when He spoke, people listened.

The writer of Hebrews tells us this:

> God, after He spoke long ago to the fathers in the prophets in many portions and in many ways, in these last days has spoken to us in His Son, whom He appointed heir of all things, through whom also He made the world (Hebrews 1:1-2).

Jesus Himself told us that God has spoken of Him in "the Law of Moses and the Prophets and the Psalms" (Luke 24:44). And God speaks in other ways than this. Romans tells us that He has spoken in His creation:

> For since the creation of the world His invisible attributes, His eternal power and divine nature, have been clearly seen, being understood through what has been made, so that they are without excuse (Romans 1:20).

He speaks through His deeds, His wonderful acts. And here is where we must listen with our eyes. We must look to see who He is.

And this is what the psalmists have been talking about. If Israel had paid attention to what God had done for them, listening to Him with their eyes, they would have known that He was faithful. They would have known that He had not abandoned them. They would have known that He would rise up in judgment against evil and vindicate the righteous.

But they weren't listening. God sent prophet after prophet to declare His Word. But Jesus rightly said that Jerusalem killed the prophets and stoned those sent to her. After Malachi, Israel had 400 years of prophetic silence. No prophet spoke to Israel audibly, and no Word was written from God.

But in those 400 years, the Scripture that was already written was the witness, the voice of God. And God still acted on Israel's behalf, speaking to them of His continuing care. After the Maccabean revolt and the defeat of the Greeks who had defiled the temple, Israel sought to cleanse the temple. There was only enough consecrated holy oil to light the lamps in the temple for one day. But according to Jewish writings, the oil lasted eight days. The commemoration of this act is called the Feast of the Dedication in the Gospel of John. Today it is called the Feast of Lights, or Hannukah, and is celebrated in December.

In this event, God was telling His people that they could not on their own bring enough light into the world, but that He Himself would bring light that would outlast their light; He would bring the Light of the World. At the birth of Jesus, there was a star for all men to see. Wise men from the east followed this star to Bethlehem. They listened with their eyes and heard God speak through the star.

Do you listen with your eyes? Do you see God speak in His wonderful deeds and know that He is still speaking today?

Does God Perform Wonders for the Dead?

∾∾∾∾

What does a loving God do for those condemned to death? When we call upon Him, does He rescue us? Does He comfort us in our affliction? What example does the Scripture give for God's lovingkindness toward those He loves?

DAY ONE

We'll study two psalms today: 87 and 88. Start by reading Psalm 87, marking key words from your bookmark as you have been doing.

Make a list of what you learned about God and the city of God, Zion. What is the message of this psalm?

Psalm 88 is a favorite of mine because it speaks far into the future from when it was written. See what you think. Mark the key words from your bookmark and also *dead*, and its synonyms, like the *grave*. I use a tombstone like this: ⌂ .

Now read Matthew 26:57–27:2 (parallel passages are Mark 14:53–15:1 and Luke 22:54–23:1).

Record themes for Psalms 87 and 88 on PSALMS AT A GLANCE.

DAYS TWO, THREE, & FOUR

Psalm 89 is a long one, so we'll take three days to cover it. Begin by reading Psalm 89 and marking key words as usual. Look for and mark time indicators, especially *forever*.

We suggest you pace yourself over the three days, taking about 17 verses a day, marking and making lists that answer the questions below. Alternatively, you can divide the psalm in half and reserve the third day for answering the questions.

List what you learned about God. What does God say He has done and will do? What does the psalmist say he will do? What questions does he ask?

What is the most important key word or concept in this psalm? Record a theme for Psalm 89 on PSALMS AT A GLANCE.

DAY FIVE

Today read Psalm 90, marking the key words from your bookmark. Notice that the superscription specifies the author and that this psalm is a prayer. Time indicators are key in this psalm.

How long has God been God? What is 1000 years like to God? Compare this with 2 Peter 3:8.

How long are our days? What do our lifespans look like to God? What does God extend to us? Are you satisfied with His lovingkindness? Should you be?

Finally, record a theme for Psalm 90 on PSALMS AT A GLANCE.

DAY SIX

Our last psalm this week is Psalm 91. Read it, marking the key words from your bookmark.

List what you learned about God. You can divide this into two categories: who He is and what He does.

What does this psalm say God will do for us? Did you know this before? Do you live in this truth today?

Finally, record a theme for Psalm 91 on PSALMS AT A GLANCE.

DAY SEVEN

 Store in your heart: Psalm 91:11-12

Read and discuss: Psalms 87–91 (Don't overcommit time to Psalm 89 because of its length.)

QUESTIONS FOR DISCUSSION OR INDIVIDUAL STUDY

- ∾ Discuss God's relationship to Jerusalem according to Psalm 87.

- ∾ Outline the prayer life of the author of Psalm 88. Then compare your prayer life to his.

- ∾ Discuss the praise of God in Psalm 89. Compare your praise life.

- ∾ Discuss what you learned about God from these psalms.

- ∾ Contrast God's perspective on time (Psalm 90) with yours.

ᴄᴏ What are the implications for making God your shelter, refuge, and fortress according to Psalm 91?

ᴄᴏ How will you apply these psalms? What changes will you make to your prayer and praise life?

Thought for the Week

Psalm 88 is one of my favorites. Each year we take a tour group to Israel, the Holy Land. One highlight of this trip is Caiaphas' house in Jerusalem. The modern site is known as the Church of St. Peter in Gallicantu, a Roman Catholic shrine built to memorialize the crowing of the rooster after Peter denied Jesus three times.

Under the church are a prison and a cistern. The prison has stone uprights that bear the signs of where rings were probably affixed to tie the hands of prisoners. From the Gospel accounts of Jesus' time at Caiaphas' house, you can imagine Him there. A short distance away is a dry cistern— a rainwater collector. It rains in the winter there, and collected water is used during the dry season from April to November.

The cistern was probably used as a holding cell for prisoners. It's more than twice the height of a man. In Jeremiah's day it was partially filled with mud. Jeremiah 38:6-13 describes the process of lowering and raising a prisoner from a cistern, using ropes and rags for padding (as happened to Jeremiah).

Today there are steps so you can go down into this cistern. We go down each year with a busload of people at a time, and a person in each group reads Psalm 88. To stand where Jesus stood nearly 2000 years ago and to read this psalm and see how applicable it was to His situation is a moving experience.

You can imagine Jesus Himself in that cistern after being beaten and mocked and spat upon by the Jews that night. You can relate to the verse that says He was reckoned among those who go down to the pit, forsaken among the dead. He was put in a dark place, the lowest pit. His acquaintances were far from Him and loathed Him. He was shut up, unable to escape. He called upon His Father.

In the morning Jesus' prayer ascended to His Father as He was released and taken to Pontius Pilate. In the awfulness of His suffering leading up to the cross, you can see how this psalm reflects that terrible night. Psalm 22 reflects the awfulness of Jesus' suffering on the cross, and the psalmist captures a similar emotion here.

The psalmist asks God questions: "Will You perform wonders for the dead?" "Will Your lovingkindness be declared in the grave?"

The answers are found in the Gospels. God did perform wonders for the dead. Jesus was resurrected, raised from the dead on the third day, declaring victory over death so that we also might be resurrected, so that death would have no hold over us. That wonder is a result of God's lovingkindness, that steadfast love extended to those in covenant with Him.

Which covenant? The New Covenant, promised in Jeremiah and Ezekiel, that God would write His law on our hearts—new hearts of malleable flesh replacing the callous hearts of stone. And He would put His Spirit within to empower us to walk in His statutes and observe His commandments. As both Jeremiah and Ezekiel state, we know this covenant is for Israel and Judah.

And the New Testament makes clear that we too are part of this covenant. According to Paul in 1 Corinthians 11, when Jesus broke the bread and drank the cup at supper the night before He was betrayed and arrested, He declared that this was the New Covenant in His blood. Paul's letter was addressed to the church in Corinth, Greece, which was comprised mostly of Gentiles. Also in that letter he says that whoever eats the bread or drinks the cup of the Lord proclaims the Lord's death until He comes. The writer of Hebrews confirms this same truth. So all who believe the gospel participate in the New Covenant.

God's lovingkindness extends to those who have the sentence of death because of sin. The wages of sin is death, and all have sinned. All men have the "sentence of death within" (2 Corinthians 1:9), but God grants the ultimate pardon and everlasting life to those who believe. That's why the Lord is the God of our salvation.

Is He yours?

Sing to the Lord
a New Song

"Sing to the Lord a new song...Proclaim good tidings of His salvation...Tell of His glory among the nations" (Psalm 96:1-3). We often sing praises from the psalms to God in worship services, but do we sing His praises outside, in public? Perhaps the tradition of Christmas caroling should be revived and expanded.

DAY ONE

Read Psalm 92 today, marking the key words on your bookmark as usual. You should notice the praise song in book 4 of Psalms—a shift in tone and content. You'll also see a shift in authorship—fewer by David and many without identified authors.

Make a list of what you learned about God that explains why it's good to give Him thanks.

What will the Lord do for the righteous? What will they do for the Lord?

Record a theme for Psalm 92 on PSALMS AT A GLANCE.

DAYS TWO & THREE

Today is another two-psalm day. Start by reading Psalm 93 (it's only five verses) and marking key words as usual. Look for time indicators. List what you learned about God. What is His relationship to the earth?

Now read Psalm 94 and mark the key words from your bookmark.

What did you learn about God and about the wicked? What end awaits the wicked? From this psalm, what is the purpose of God's judgment?

Record themes for Psalms 93 and 94 on PSALMS AT A GLANCE.

DAY FOUR

Read Psalm 95 today and mark the key words from your bookmark. How are we to approach God according to this psalm? Why? What did you learn about God?

You might recognize the praise chorus of verses 6 and 7. What do these verses teach about the physical expression of worship? And what place does the heart have?

Record a theme for Psalm 95 on PSALMS AT A GLANCE.

DAY FIVE

The details in Psalm 96:1-13 and 1 Chronicles 16:23-33

are identical—part of Jewish worship after the ark of the covenant was brought to Jerusalem. In 1 Chronicles 16 and 2 Samuel 6, we read about David placing the ark of the covenant in the tent in Jerusalem that he had made for it. Bringing the ark of the covenant to Jerusalem was a major event in the history of worship in Israel. Philistines had captured it in battle before Saul was king, but after troubling experiences with it, they returned it to Israel, and it stayed in the house of Abinadab in Kiriath-jearim. When you have time, read 1 Samuel 4:12–7:2 for that story. You can also read 2 Samuel 6 and its parallel passage, 1 Chronicles 15–16, for the story of David bringing the ark to Jerusalem.

Once the ark was in the tent in Jerusalem, David assigned Asaph and his relatives to give thanks to the Lord. First Chronicles 16:22-33 and Psalm 96:1-13 are part of that thanksgiving.

With that background, read Psalm 96 today and mark the key words from your bookmark. What did you learn about singing, rejoicing, and worship? If you made a list yesterday about worship, add what you learned from this psalm to it.

What things are to be proclaimed or foretold? To whom should these things be sung?

What did you learn about judgment from this psalm?

Record a theme for Psalm 96 on PSALMS AT A GLANCE.

DAY SIX

Read Psalm 97 today and mark the key words from your bookmark.

Make a list of what you learned about God and relate it to rejoicing. Compare verse 6 to Romans 1:19-20.

If we love the Lord, what should be our attitude toward evil? What do we rejoice over?

Finally, record a theme for Psalm 97 on PSALMS AT A GLANCE.

DAY SEVEN

Store in your heart: Psalm 95:6-7
Read and discuss: Psalms 92–97

QUESTIONS FOR DISCUSSION OR INDIVIDUAL STUDY

- ∽ Discuss reasons for worshipping God from these psalms.

- ∽ Discuss ways we should worship according to these psalms.

- ∽ What did you learn about singing and rejoicing? What do we declare in our singing? To whom do we sing?

- ∽ What is the relationship between judgment and worship? What's the purpose of judgment?

- ∽ Discuss what you learned about God.

- ∽ What applications will you make this week? Do you need to change anything in your worship?

THOUGHT FOR THE WEEK

All 150 psalms proclaim truth about God. Some are prayers, some praises, some songs…all designed to worship

Him. In this week's psalms, though, we get specific ideas about what God considers worship.

Back in Psalm 40 we learned that God prefers obedience to sacrifice:

> Sacrifice and meal offering You have not desired;
> My ears You have opened;
> Burnt offering and sin offering You have not required.
> Then I said, "Behold, I come;
> In the scroll of the book it is written of me.
> I delight to do Your will, O my God;
> Your Law is within my heart."
> (Psalm 40:6-8)

The conclusion of this is that life is worship if it is a life of obedience to God.

This week we have learned some things about the physical expression of worship. Psalm 95 calls us to bow down and kneel before the Lord. The Hebrew word translated "worship" here usually means to bow or make low, to humble oneself. Following the Hebrew word translated "bow down," the emphasis is humbling oneself *and* bowing down. The Hebrew word translated "kneel" here shows us that both bowing and kneeling express humility. What's important to understand is that posture is not the same as humility. Anyone with power to inflict pain or death can compel someone to kneel or bow. Fear of punishment is not the same motive as respectful love.

There's a story about a little girl who was standing up in the pew during a church worship service and her father told her to sit down. She complied but said, "I may be sitting down on the outside, but on the inside I'm standing up!" This is a good example of a form of obedience without the heart for it. And that's the point of bowing down or kneeling. If it's not from a heart of humility before God, it's just a ritual. What God wants is humility.

Elsewhere in these psalms we also find that we are to sing *joyfully* to the Lord. I'm amazed at people in worship services who don't sing at all and also those who do sing but look as if they're in pain. Singing in worship is supposed to be joyful, not grudging, not painful, and certainly not a talent contest to see who's best. Just because we can't sing well doesn't mean we shouldn't sing joyfully. Psalm 95:1 says to sing for joy and then says to shout joyfully, so I'm convinced talent is not the issue.

Then we learn what we're to bring God in these joyful acts. We're to come before His presence with thanksgiving and either shout joyfully with psalms or make joyful noises. An alternate translation adds the accompaniment of musical instruments. Psalm 92:3 commands the use of the ten-stringed lute, the harp, and the lyre, and the music is to be resounding. Today we generally use other instruments. When David organized worship for the temple Solomon would build, he specified lyres, harps, cymbals, and singing. Psalm 98 adds trumpets and horns.

We also learn from these psalms the content of worship: thanksgiving and proclaiming good tidings of God's salvation, glory, wonderful deeds, splendor and majesty, strength and beauty, creative power, righteousness, and lovingkindness.

We also learn that the whole earth should praise God. The heavens, earth, mountains, seas, islands, fields, and trees are all called to rejoice and sing for joy. All God created should praise Him for who He is and what He has done.

That's the kind of worship Psalms describes. God commands everything He created to make that response. Is this a picture of your worship?

BLESS THE LORD, O MY SOUL

⚬⚬⚬⚬

"Bless the LORD, O my soul, and all that is within me, bless His holy name" (Psalm 103:1). Do you remember the command to love the Lord your God? How are we to do that? With all our heart, all our mind, all our soul, and all our strength. All that is within me. That's how we're to *bless* the Lord too. If we love Him this way, we should bless Him this way.

DAY ONE

Two psalms today. Start with Psalm 98, marking key words from your bookmark as you have been doing.

Make a list of what you learned about praising God. Use the 5 W's and an H.

Now read Psalm 99, again marking key words from your bookmark. When you're done, make a list about God. This psalm doesn't tell us to praise Him, but it does list who He is and what He has done that makes Him worthy of praise and worship.

Record themes for Psalms 98 and 99 on PSALMS AT A GLANCE.

DAY TWO

Today is another two-psalm day. Start by reading Psalm 100 and marking the key words. Psalm 100 contains more words for modern praise choruses. It's short and full of instruction to praise. List what you learn about God.

Now read and mark Psalm 101 the same way. This psalm of David focuses more on how he will *live* in praise than what he will say, sing, or shout. List what he says he will do and then ask yourself if you do these things too.

Record themes for Psalms 100 and 101 on PSALMS AT A GLANCE.

DAY THREE

Read Psalm 102 today and mark the key words from your bookmark. This psalm may remind you of earlier ones in the way the psalmist asks God not to hide His face in days of distress.

Note the psalmist's situation. What is he doing? How does he feel? What are his questions about God?

What does the psalmist vow to remember? What should you and I remember about God? (List truths about God from this psalm.) What are your insights about verse 18? Who do you think these "people yet to be created" are?

Record a theme for Psalm 102 on PSALMS AT A GLANCE.

DAY FOUR

Read Psalm 103 today, marking key words. Again the first verse opens with a familiar praise chorus. This is another good psalm from which to extract and list truths about God. These will show you why David blesses God.

List the contrasts between man and God. The sentiments are similar to those at the end of the previous psalm with respect to the earth. Also make a short list of who should bless God.

Finally, record a theme for Psalm 103 on PSALMS AT A GLANCE.

DAYS FIVE & SIX

Psalm 104 is a little longer than 103, so we're going to take two days to cover it. Take it one bite at a time. Spread your study over two days and take your time to soak in what this psalm declares about God creating the earth. Start by reading through the psalm, marking key words. Then list in your notebook what you learned about God one paragraph at a time.

Finally, record a theme for Psalm 104 on PSALMS AT A GLANCE.

DAY SEVEN

 Store in your heart: Psalm 103:1

Read and discuss: Psalms 98–104

QUESTIONS FOR DISCUSSION OR INDIVIDUAL STUDY

- ∾ Discuss what you learned about God that is worthy of thanks and praise. You might break down this discussion into categories: what He has done for you, His creation, and what He will do in the future. These are just ideas, so feel free to create your own categories. Even a discussion of categorizing is fruitful.

- ∾ What did you learn about worshipping God— singing, shouting, giving thanks? Use the 5 W's and an H as your springboard for this discussion.

- ∾ Now spend some time discussing how your life sings praises to God.

- ∾ What have you learned that will impact your life? What truths will affect your relationship with God? What lessons will you commit to live out?

THOUGHT FOR THE WEEK

"Bless the LORD, O my soul, and all that is within me, bless His holy name" (Psalm 103:1). Why "all that is within me"? Because that's the way to love Him: with all your heart, soul, mind, and strength. Why does He deserve our all? Because of who He is, what He has done, and what He will do.

Sometimes we forget exactly what God has done. We may rattle off the right biblical propositions, such as "He is the Creator" or "He is the Redeemer," but do we stop and meditate on what these mean? Psalms 103 and 104 really help us. In Psalm 103 David outlines things we should remember about our Redeemer. We should spend some time meditating on these things, not just reading, marking key words, and moving on.

David tells us to forget *none* of God's benefits. That's a key point. He benefits us. How? By pardoning all our iniquities—every one, past, present, and future. He heals our diseases. He's the Great Physician. By His stripes we are healed. His atoning death paid the price for our sin so we don't have to pay it. He dies so we can live. We are healed from the disease of sin, and we are redeemed from the pit of death. He bought us out of the slave market of sin and adopted us as sons, taking our filthy (sinful) rags and clothing us with the garments of salvation, the robe of righteousness from Christ, His Son. He set a crown on our heads with His lovingkindness and compassion. He satisfies us with good things, and our "youth is renewed like the eagle." He reinvigorates us with life.

Have you forgotten these things? Are you feeling tired and run-down? Perhaps it's time to stop and take stock of what you have in Jesus. The Lord performs righteous deeds and judgments for all those who are oppressed. If you're feeling oppressed, turn to Jesus for refreshing. Take a break from the grind of daily living and find refreshment in the Lord. Setting aside regular time in the Word of God and coming together with other believers for worship will help you find refreshment in the midst of the daily grind. We need to rehearse the words that tell us God is compassionate and gracious, slow to anger and abounding in lovingkindness. We need to hear that message because people aren't that way, at least not all the time. But God is that way *all the time.* He knows our frame and is mindful that we are dust. He has compassion on His children, those who believe and fear Him. So we join His angels, His hosts, and all His works and bless Him.

Sometimes we also need to step back from our daily routine and soak in God's creation and praise Him for that. This can be difficult for those of us living in cities that crowd out trees and mountains. And we forget that God holds even these structures together by created things. Man didn't invent or create gravity. Nor did he create mechanical and chemical properties or even colors. Man rearranges things God created. He shapes them into things we can use and admire, enjoy or abuse, but God alone is the creator of all things, "both in the heavens and on earth, visible and invisible" (Colossians 1:16).

Sometimes we need to get out into the country to admire God's creation. We need to look at clouds and water, feel wind, listen to thunder. We need to gaze at mountains and valleys and consider the habitations God created and the harmonies in these places. Deserts, rain forests, farm land, prairies, and swamps are all part of God's creation. In each habitat, different creatures exist, thrive, wither, and die. And God made them all. He provides food and water for all to grow. Fish, birds, animals, plants, and man all take their sustenance from what God created. Man may rule creation, organizing the growing of things for food, but God created it. God created day and night by placing the earth on a rotating axis and seasons by revolving the earth around the sun. God alone makes the earth shake, the rains fall, and the winds blow. He alone created harmony and dispersed it through the earth. Seeing all this, let every creature bless His holy name.

The psalms help us draw back and remember these things. Even if we don't have time to go and see these things today, the psalmist transports us to the place of remembrance. In our minds we can picture what God has done, what He has created, and what He has done to redeem. Similarly, our minds can picture His future. We can't physically see it, but we can imagine it. Words take us to these places. Jesus is coming! He will judge the earth and all its inhabitants. Created nature itself will share the freedom of the children of God (Romans 8:21).

We can't see this future, but we can believe and thank God for revealing it to us. We can sing praises to Him for securing *our* future with His unchanging nature.

"Bless the LORD, O my soul, and all that is within me"— my heart, mind, soul, and strength—"bless His holy name."

OH GIVE THANKS TO THE LORD, FOR HE IS GOOD

Rowewe

The goodness of God is described as everlasting loving-kindness. *Lovingkindness* points to covenant love, love God gives for the benefit of the recipient. *Everlasting* makes this love steadfast.

DAYS ONE & TWO

This week we'll cover three psalms, two days for each. Today and tomorrow we'll study Psalm 105.

You may recall the story of David bringing the ark of the covenant to Jerusalem. We discussed it when we studied Psalm 96. The story included Asaph and his relatives and their thanksgiving for David's directive. Psalm 105:1-15 is part of this thanksgiving. The first 15 verses of Psalm 105 are the same text as 1 Chronicles 16:8-22, so we know that part of this psalm originated with that event.

Start by reading Psalm 105, marking key words from your bookmark. Divide your study time into two days. It may take you one day just to read and mark and another to make pertinent lists and answer questions.

Make a list of what you learn about God—what He has done and His character.

Covenants were mentioned in previous psalms, sometimes with respect to the law. What do you learn about covenants in this psalm?

Like others, this psalm gives a history of Israel and God's faithfulness. From the historical context of when the first 15 verses were written, why do you think it's important to review this history again?

Record a theme for Psalm 105 on PSALMS AT A GLANCE.

DAYS THREE & FOUR

Read Psalm 106, marking key words as usual.

List what you learned about Israel. Psalm 105 included praise for the mighty works God did for Israel. What does this psalm talk about?

Despite His people's actions, what did God do for them? Do you see how a covenant is important in this psalm?

What did you learn about God? From this psalm, what is the purpose of God's judgment?

Record a theme for Psalm 106 on PSALMS AT A GLANCE.

DAYS FIVE & SIX

We begin the last of the five books of Psalms today.

Psalms 106 and 107 begin with the same words: "Oh give thanks to the LORD, for He is good."

Read Psalm 107 today and mark the key words from your bookmark. Also look for and mark key repeated phrases. They are unique to this psalm, so you don't need to add them to your bookmark, but they will help you understand the message.

Note the various situations in which God gives help. What should God's people thank Him for?

Record a theme for Psalm 107 on PSALMS AT A GLANCE.

DAY SEVEN

 Store in your heart: Psalm 107:1

Read and discuss: Psalms 105–107

QUESTIONS FOR DISCUSSION OR INDIVIDUAL STUDY

∞ Discuss historical events Israel should thank God for.

∞ How do covenants fit in the relationship between Israel and God? How do the themes of sin and redemption relate to thanksgiving and praise to God?

∞ What did you learn that will impact your life? What truths will affect your relationship with God? What lessons will you commit to live out?

THOUGHT FOR THE WEEK

God's lovingkindness, we said earlier, is everlasting, so

any covenant that contains it is as immutable as the character of the Covenant Maker. If an immutable God makes a covenant, He won't break it; in fact, He *can't*. If God's love is part of that covenant, it won't end. God is immutably faithful to the subjects of His covenants. How comforting!

In the psalms, we've seen the term *covenant* almost 20 times now. The rest of the psalms include only three more references. Psalm 105 contains a clear reference to God's covenant with Abraham. (If you want to know more about God's covenants, call Precept Ministries International at 1-800-763-8280 or log on to www.precept.org for available study guides.)

As the text says, God made an everlasting covenant with Abraham. He has kept it to date and will keep it into eternity. He confirmed this by oath to Abraham, Isaac, and Jacob, three generations. In it He promised the land of Canaan for an everlasting inheritance. The rest of the psalm details God's keeping this promise. Psalm 106:45 relates to the fulfillment of this promise too. It predicts that Israel will be released from captivity to return and repossess its promised land.

The Abrahamic covenant promises more than land, so when it's referred to, it's important to understand the "rest of the story." Genesis 12; 15; 17 and Galatians 3 give us important details.

It includes descendants as numerous as the stars in heaven—a great nation. It promises that those who bless Abraham and his nation will be blessed, and those who curse them will be cursed. It promises that in Abraham, all families of the earth will be blessed. This will occur by means of a descendant (seed) from his own body, through Sarah, his wife. Finally, this covenant will be everlasting.

Abraham believed God, and this faith was "reckoned" (counted, accounted, credited) to him as righteousness.

Galatians 3 makes clear that those who share his faith are his descendents. Those who believe the promised seed of Abraham receive God's covenant promise and lovingkindness to Abraham. Galatians 3 also makes clear that God did not promise many seeds, but one seed, that is Christ. So all who believe in Christ are heirs of the promise of Abraham, including Gentiles (those who are not Jews). You and I are part of that covenant promise of God.

In making this covenant, God took the form of a smoking oven and flaming torch and passed between the pieces of flesh Abraham had laid out. This reflected a cultural custom of cutting an animal in half, laying the two pieces opposite one another, and walking through them, saying, "If I break this covenant, let this be done to me." Since God passed through the pieces, not Abraham, and God cannot lie, His covenant is inviolable. God the Covenant Maker will keep His covenant.

Jacob, Abraham's grandson, took his family to Egypt to find food. After a long time—430 years—God brought the nation of Israel, the descendants of Jacob, to Mount Sinai in the wilderness and made a covenant with them, which we call the law. Consisting of ten commandments and nearly 600 additional ordinances, this law (according to Galatians 3) was *added* to the Abrahamic covenant; it did not replace it. The law defined sin and provided methods (rituals) to approach a holy God and live a holy life. The purpose of this law was to be a tutor to lead God's people to Christ to be justified (declared righteous) by faith. Now that Jesus and His atonement have arrived, God's people have no need for the tutor.

In Jeremiah and Ezekiel, God declares that one day He will make a New Covenant with Israel and Jacob. The Gospels, 1 Corinthians, and Hebrews all state that this New Covenant is entered into through faith in Christ. This is the covenant in which all who believe the gospel are now made righteous and have become heirs of the Abrahamic covenant promises. Righteousness has always been by faith, as we saw in Abraham's response to the covenant. It was never by works, by the law, which was intended only to lead to faith.

So the everlasting covenant to Abraham looks forward to the New Covenant, with the same promise of everlasting life for those who believe. And in this way, all of us from all the nations of the earth who believe in the gospel of Jesus Christ fulfill God's promise that Abraham will be made into a great nation and that all other nations will be blessed in him.

You are blessed! Perhaps you should thank God and sing praise to Him as the psalmists did!

BE EXALTED, O GOD, ABOVE THE HEAVENS

ᘓᘉᘓᘉ

Why should the Lord be exalted above the heavens? He is creator of all things, so He should be exalted above all things. Yet men make idols with their hands and exalt them above the God who created them. Why?

DAY ONE

Read Psalm 108 today, marking key words from your bookmark. Mark geographical references and check them against the map on the next page.

Make a list of what you learned about God.

Now, what issue provokes this psalm? What's going on? What does the psalmist ask God to do? Why? What did you learn about God that might explain why the psalmist asks God to act?

Record a theme for Psalm 108 on PSALMS AT A GLANCE.

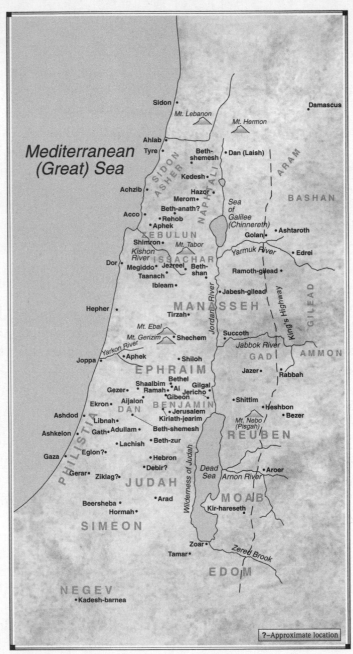

THE PROMISED LAND

DAYS TWO & THREE

Today and tomorrow we'll cover another long psalm, so spread your study over two days. Read Psalm 109 and mark key words as usual. List what you learned about the wicked. What does the psalmist ask God to do to the wicked?

List what you learned about the psalmist's condition. In contrast with what he asks God to do to the wicked, what does the psalmist ask God to do for him?

Record a theme for Psalm 109 on PSALMS AT A GLANCE.

DAY FOUR

Our plan today is to study two relatively short psalms. Read Psalm 110 today and mark the key words from your bookmark.

Now read Matthew 22:41-46, Acts 2:31-36, and Hebrews 5:5-10. How does the New Testament interpret Psalm 110?

Now read Psalm 111 and mark key words as usual. Make a list of what you learned about God. The truth about "the fear of the LORD" in verse 10 is also found extensively in Job and Proverbs.

Record themes for Psalms 110 and 111 on PSALMS AT A GLANCE.

DAY FIVE

We'll study two psalms again today. Start with Psalm

112. Read and mark this psalm as you have before. What is true about the man who fears the Lord? By contrast, what is true about the wicked? How do the two kinds of people relate?

Now read and mark Psalm 113. What should God's servants praise Him for?

Finally, record themes for Psalms 112 and 113 on PSALMS AT A GLANCE.

DAY SIX

For our last day of study this week, we will again cover two psalms. Start with Psalm 114, marking as usual. How is the power of God over creation revealed in this psalm?

The sea mentioned in verse 3 is the Red Sea, which God parted when He took Israel out of Egypt—the people of "strange language" (see Exodus 14 for an account). God also parted the Jordan River when He brought Israel into the promised land of Canaan (see Joshua 3 for this account). Mountains quaked at Mount Sinai in Exodus 19, and a rock produced water in Exodus 17. Miracles sometimes accompany significant events.

Now read and mark Psalm 115. Mark *idols* and pronouns that refer to them, but don't add either to your bookmark. (I use a little statue of a man like an Oscar.)

List what you learned about idols and then about God. The "house of Aaron" are the priests. Contrast idols with God (from the text). How does creation relate to God and to idols?

Finally, record themes for Psalms 114 and 115 on PSALMS AT A GLANCE.

DAY SEVEN

Store in your heart: Psalm 108:5
Read and discuss: Psalms 108–115

QUESTIONS FOR DISCUSSION OR INDIVIDUAL STUDY

~ What issues provide the setting for Psalm 108 and 109? Considering each psalm separately, what's going on? What does the psalmist ask God to do? Why? What did you learn about God that might explain why the psalmist asks God to act?

~ How does Psalm 110 speak of Jesus?

~ What did you learn about God from Psalm 111?

~ What did you learn about the righteous man in Psalm 112?

~ What did Psalm 113 teach you about God that you should praise Him for?

~ Discuss the implications of the events in Psalm 114. How do they lead to praise and worship of God?

~ Contrast idols with God from Psalm 115.

~ What have you learned from these psalms that will impact your life? What truths will affect your relationship with God? What lessons will you commit to live out?

THOUGHT FOR THE WEEK

Psalm 123 says that God is enthroned in the heavens. Through Isaiah the prophet, God declares, "Heaven is My throne and the earth is My footstool. Where then is a house you could build for Me? And where is a place that I may rest?" (Isaiah 66:1).

Throughout Psalms we've seen God as the Creator of the heavens and the earth, so He transcends the physical heavens and earth we see. And His throne in the heavens must transcend the creation. That's why astronauts have not seen the throne of God when in space.

We also know that Jesus, God's only begotten Son, God who became flesh and dwelt among us, ascended into heaven after 40 days of ministry on earth following His resurrection from the dead. Hebrews and 1 Peter teach that Jesus sat down at the right hand of God.

The right hand, which is dominant in most people, is the side of authority and power. The same hand both points a weapon and extends friendship and peace. The one who sits at the right hand is the chief deputy, next in line of authority. From this concept we get our phrase *right-hand man*—the most trusted, valuable, utilized assistant.

Jesus, then, sitting at the right hand of God, is the Father's ultimate Agent. What role does He have? Job said, "Even now, behold, my witness is in heaven, and my advocate is on high." John reinforces this: "If anyone sins, we have an Advocate with the Father, Jesus Christ the righteous." We need an advocate, someone who pleads our case to the Father, because we have an adversary, the devil who prowls about like a roaring lion, seeking to devour. He's called "the accuser of our brethren" in Revelation.

But our Advocate is at God's right hand. Satan will accuse us as guilty of sin and unworthy of mercy according to strict legal justice. But our Advocate will stretch out His nail-pierced hands and show the Father that the penalty has already been paid, and the Father will look at the accused, you and me, and see that we are clothed with the righteous-ness of Christ. He will tell Satan our sins are forgiven; we will live, not die.

This great drama unfolds over all the centuries that Jesus sits at the right hand of God. Psalm 110 says that He sits there until His enemies are made a footstool for His feet. First Corinthians 15 declares that Jesus will reign until He has put all His enemies under His feet. And the last enemy to be abolished is death.

In Revelation we read about a "great white throne" judg-ment after Jesus' millennial reign, when death and Hades are thrown into the lake of fire, the second death. Then we have the description of the new heavens and new earth, in which there is no more death.

Jesus is a priest forever according to the order of Melchizedek, one without beginning or end, with no mother or father. For Jesus is God, not a created being. Psalm 110 can't be speaking of David because Jesus says in it David refers to the Christ as his Lord.

This is the good news. David hits the nail on the head here. No man can deliver us from the power of the enemy. Only the God-man, Jesus, can deliver us from "him who had the power of death, that is, the devil" (Hebrews 2:14). God had to become flesh to do that, and God did in the person of Jesus. As David prays in Psalm 108, "Oh give us help against the adversary, for deliverance by man is in vain." The Lord is our help!

Following His victory over death, Jesus opened the way for us to enter the very throne room of God. In the temple, no one but the High Priest could enter the Holy of Holies to stand before the ark of the covenant on which was the mercy seat, where God Himself met with man. But at Jesus' death, the veil was torn in two, opening the way. This great

High Priest, not descended from Aaron but of the order of Melchizedek, now stands before God's throne ministering continually. Now we can boldly approach the throne of grace.

That's what Psalm 110 points to. Rejoice and praise the Lord! Give Him thanks!

THIS IS THE LORD'S DOING

The psalmists cried for redemption, and Israel read those psalms for nearly 1000 years. But when the Lord provided the Redeemer, did they recognize that day and rejoice, or did they reject it? What about you? Do you recognize God's answer to your cry when it comes in a way you didn't expect?

DAY ONE

Read Psalm 116 today, marking key words from your bookmark as usual.

Make a list of what you learned about God. Also list why the psalmist loves the Lord and how he plans to serve the Lord.

Record a theme for Psalm 116 on PSALMS AT A GLANCE.

DAYS TWO & THREE

Today is another two-psalm day, including the shortest psalm, just two verses. Start by reading Psalm 117 and marking key words. What two things about the Lord are worthy of praise? And who should praise Him for these?

Now read Psalm 118 and mark the key words from your bookmark. Also mark key repeated phrases. What did you learn about God?

Jesus interpreted verses 22 and 23 in Matthew 21:42-44. Start at verse 33 for the larger context. Also read 1 Peter 2:4-8.

Verses 23 and 24 are often quoted apart from the context of verse 22. In fact, all three go together. How do they relate to the main theme of this Psalm?

Record themes for Psalms 117 and 118 on PSALMS AT A GLANCE.

DAY FOUR

We've come to the longest psalm, 176 verses. We'll finish up this week with part of our study, and then spend all next week on it too. One interesting feature is that this psalm is an acrostic in Hebrew—22 strophes (paragraphs) of eight verses each. The first word of each verse in each strophe starts with the same letter, continuing in order of the 22 letters of the Hebrew alphabet. So in verses 1-8, for example, the first word of each verse starts with the first letter of the Hebrew alphabet, *aleph*. In the second strophe, verses 9-16, each verse starts with a word starting with the second letter of the Hebrew alphabet, *bet*. In most Bibles, the alphabet is listed with the English text, so you can learn Hebrew letters by studying this psalm. (Now if someone would just pronounce them for you!)

The psalm is so long we won't read it through in one day. At the end of next week you'll determine a theme for the entire psalm, so take notes about the content paragraph by paragraph as you go. It will make sense at the end.

You'll have to pay careful attention to synonyms in this psalm. The *word* of God is key to every verse, but it appears as *law, testimonies, precepts, statutes,*[19] *commandments, ordinances,*[20] *judgments,*[21] even *ways.* Context is a key to discerning these in the translation you use.

Start by reading through verses 1-8, marking the key words from your bookmark and references to God's Word. List in your notebook what you learned.

What pattern do you see in verses 1-8? Are there other key repeated words?

Now continue this pattern. To keep moving along at a good pace, cover at least 16 verses each day. We're only going to take these three days and all of next week, a total of nine study days, to cover this psalm, so one pattern that will work is to study 16 verses in five of those days and 24 verses in the other four.

For today, cover the first 16 verses.

DAY FIVE

Follow the study directions from yesterday but cover verses 17 through 40.

DAY SIX

Follow the study directions from day 4, studying verses 41-56.

DAY SEVEN

Store in your heart: Psalm 118:22-24

Read and discuss: Psalms 116–118 (We'll leave all of Psalm 119 to next week.)

QUESTIONS FOR DISCUSSION OR INDIVIDUAL STUDY

- ᴥ Discuss what it's like to cry out to God and then hear His answer. How do you react when this happens?

- ᴥ Share examples of answered prayer from your lives.

- ᴥ What truths about God and His works cause you to rejoice?

- ᴥ What does "take refuge in God" mean to you?

- ᴥ What does "You are *my* God" mean to you?

- ᴥ What have you learned from these psalms that will impact your life? What truths will affect your relationship with God? What lessons will you commit to live out?

THOUGHT FOR THE WEEK

You may have heard someone say this: "God always answers prayer. His answer could be yes, no, or wait." This can be comforting or frustrating, but sometimes answers are completely unexpected. What we think an answer should be is not always what God gives.

A friend of mine prayed for 25 years for her lost husband to come to faith. He played the religious game and said the right Christian words, but he didn't believe, and she knew it.

He was a business success and enjoyed the fruits of his labor in pleasurable activities.

Then one day he had a stroke. In the hospital room, in the midst of what appeared to be a terrible tragedy, he came to believe in Jesus. And the Lord revealed to him this truth: He had always thought that if God didn't want him to have his "toys" (possessions), God would take them away. He never imagined that God would take away his ability to use them. God answered prayers for his salvation in a totally unexpected way.

Israel cried out to God for a Messiah. They longed to experience the redemption that was promised as far back as the garden of Eden. But when God sent the Messiah (the Christ) in the form of a little baby born in a manger, a baby who grew up among them and showed the world that Israel didn't live according to God's covenant promises, they rejected Him. They rejected His plan. They didn't accept Jesus of Nazareth as the anointed one, the Messiah, the Christ.

David dreamed of and Solomon built a temple for God made of stones. It was destroyed by the Babylonians in 586 BC. The remnant that returned from the Babylonian captivity rebuilt the temple, but it was no match for the original. Then around 19 BC, Herod the Great, the king the Romans installed over Israel, began an improvement program for this temple. He wanted it to equal or surpass the beauty of Solomon's temple. But God planned Jesus to be the cornerstone of a *new kind* of building, a new kind of temple, made up of believers.

Paul wrote this in his letter to the Ephesians, speaking of Gentiles (non-Jews):

> So then you are no longer strangers and aliens,
> but you are fellow citizens with the saints, and
> are of God's household, having been built on the

foundation of the apostles and prophets, Christ Jesus Himself being the corner stone, in whom the whole building, being fitted together, is growing into a holy temple in the Lord, in whom you also are being built together into a dwelling of God in the Spirit (Ephesians 2:19-22).

And as you saw in your study, 1 Peter 2:4-10 continues this thought. Peter quotes Psalm 118:22 and explains that Jesus was rejected by the builders (the Jews):

And coming to Him as to a living stone which has been rejected by men, but is choice and precious in the sight of God, you also, as living stones, are being built up as a spiritual house for a holy priesthood, to offer up spiritual sacrifices acceptable to God through Jesus Christ. For this is contained in Scripture: "Behold, I lay in Zion a choice stone, a precious corner stone, and he who believes in Him will not be disappointed." This precious value, then, is for you who believe; but for those who disbelieve, "The stone which the builders rejected, this became the very corner stone," and, "A stone of stumbling and a rock of offense"; for they stumble because they are disobedient to the word, and to this doom they were also appointed.

But you are a chosen race, a royal priesthood, a holy nation, a people for God's own possession, so that you may proclaim the excellencies of Him who has called you out of darkness into His marvelous light; for you once were not a people, but now you are the people of God;

you had not received mercy, but now you have
received mercy.

God did something unexpected in Jesus—He atoned for
the sins of the world, reaching out to Gentiles. According to
Matthew 21:33-44, Jesus said that non-Jews will inherit the
vineyard (the metaphor used in verses 33-41). He quotes
Psalm 118:23-24: "This is marvelous in our eyes." What is?
A temple of God made up of believers with Jesus as the cornerstone and the apostles and prophets as the foundation.
Believers are living stones built into a spiritual house and
priesthood, Paul says.

The stone temple and Levitical priesthood were not the
final plan of God, but the Jews rejected the idea of a spiritual
temple and priesthood.

THY WORD IS A LAMP TO MY FEET

ᘓᘓᘓᘓ

This song title comes from Psalm 119:105 (KJV): "Thy word is a lamp unto my feet, and a light unto my path." God's Word shows us how to walk and not stumble, how to live a life according to His precepts, commandments, and teachings. Psalm 119 is 176 verses of instruction about the value of God's Word in our lives.

DAY ONE

Go back and read the directions for day 4 from last week if you need review. We'll continue the pattern of marking key words, covering either 16 or 24 verses a day. Note the theme for each set of 8 verses in your Bible or notebook. By the end of this week you'll have 22 themes listed, from which you'll discern a common theme to record on PSALMS AT A GLANCE.

Today, we'll cover verses 57-80.

DAY TWO

Follow the same direction for verses 81-96.

DAY THREE

Today's assignment is verses 97-120.

DAY FOUR

Study verses 121-136 today.

DAY FIVE

Verses 137 to 160 are today's treasure.

DAY SIX

Two strophes (verses 161-176), and then we're done!
Finally, record a theme for Psalm 119 on PSALMS AT A
GLANCE. Good job! Thank you for persevering through this
long psalm. It was worth it, wasn't it!

DAY SEVEN

 Store in your heart: Psalm 119:105
Read and discuss: Psalm 119

QUESTIONS FOR DISCUSSION OR INDIVIDUAL STUDY

- ∾ Discuss the importance of God's Word.

- ∾ What are the nuances among the various English synonyms for *word*?

- ∾ Discuss the psalmist's response to God's Word. Then discuss your own response. How do they differ? How are they the same? How do you identify with the psalmist?

- ∾ What have you learned from Psalm 119 that will impact your life? What truths will affect your relationship with God? What lessons will you commit to live out?

THOUGHT FOR THE WEEK

The psalmist wrote, "Thy word is a lamp unto my feet, and a light unto my path" (Psalm 119:105 KJV).

The prophet Isaiah declared, "The people who walk in darkness will see a great light; those who live in a dark land, the light will shine on them" (Isaiah 9:2).

And the apostle John wrote in his Gospel,

> In the beginning was the Word, and the Word was with God, and the Word was God. In Him was life, and the life was the Light of men. The Light shines in the darkness, and the darkness did not comprehend it (John 1:1,4-5).

Jesus, the Word of God, God Himself, is the Light that shines in the darkness, the light Isaiah prophesied to Israel, the land in darkness. As we saw last week, He was unexpected. God delivered on His promise, but it wasn't what Israel thought would happen. But this week as we pored over Psalm 119, the one verse that stuck out to me was verse 105.

. The idea of light dispelling darkness runs throughout the Scripture. Paul wrote to the Colossians that we were rescued from the kingdom of darkness, Satan's kingdom. We speak today in everyday language about darkness and light representing evil and good. In the Star Wars movies, the hero is dressed in white, and the villain (in black) invites the hero to come over to the "dark side." In the early years of Western movies, the good guys wore the white hats, and the bad guys wore black.

When the good guys triumphed over the bad guys, we saw this same phenomenon—light dispelling darkness. Throughout the ages this idea of dark representing evil and light representing good has come from biblical images. Without physical light we stumble, we bump into things, we fall into holes and hurt ourselves. Light exposes hidden dangers. Dark hides things we don't want others to see, and light exposes them for all to see. Of course, some things done in the dark can be good, and not having them exposed provides safety. But those doing evil prefer darkness to light, as John wrote:

> This is the judgment, that the Light has come into the world, and men loved the darkness rather than the Light, for their deeds were evil. For everyone who does evil hates the Light, and does not come to the Light for fear that his deeds will be exposed. But he who practices the truth comes to the Light, so that his deeds may be manifested as having been wrought in God (John 3:19-21).

So if our motivation is to practice truth and we want the

world to see that our deeds have been worked by God, we need light. And where do we get that light? From the Word of God. That's what the psalmist said for 176 verses—the Word of God is vital for life. The commandments, precepts, and instructions God's Word provides are all vital for our lives if we want to be effective as Christ's ambassadors.

Since the darkness and light we've been discussing are spiritual, not physical, where do we find answers to spiritual matters? In Ouija boards, crystal balls, palms of our hands, tarot cards, or bumps on our heads? Many people must think so, or these things wouldn't flourish in our society. In some parts of the world, answers to life are found by casting bones or reading signs in goat entrails (don't laugh, I've seen it!). Witch doctors are consulted, candles are lit, and incense is burned.

These things don't bring light. They belong to the darkness. If they didn't, God wouldn't have forbidden them in both Testaments. Witchcraft, divination, sorcery, mediums, and spiritists...these practices don't rely on God and His Word for answers. These spiritual powers and authorities are rebelling against God. Although their judgment is certain and their power limited, they nonetheless exist and have power to deceive.

God's Word exposes the deeds of the dark powers and of men who love evil and hate good. God's Word shows us the paths of righteousness—the path of sanctification to become Christlike in our thought, speech, and actions. God's Word has supernatural power to conform us to the image of Christ. That's why in Ezekiel we learned that God writes His Word on new hearts of flesh so that transformation begins on the inside. Elsewhere the Scripture talks about our hearts being circumcised (Deuteronomy 10:16; 30:6; Jeremiah 4:4).

We receive a new heart of flesh with God's truth inscribed

on it. God the Holy Spirit indwells us, giving us the power to live according to God's Word. But we must continue to fill our hearts and minds with all God's Word and live by it to be presented before Him spotless and blameless. We must walk in the light of God's Word that we have read and studied.

FROM WHERE SHALL MY HELP COME?

∾∿∾∿

When God's people were serious enough about worship to trek all the way to the temple in Jerusalem for one of the annual feasts, where did they look for help on their journey? Where do *you* look today? Do you look to the Lord for your help?

DAY ONE

This week we will study a series of 15 psalms called the songs of *ascents*—a term that describes the purpose of these psalms: to recite when worshippers ascended to the temple in Jerusalem for the feasts. *Ascents* refers partly to the topography of the Holy Land. Jerusalem sits on top of the central ridge of mountains that slope downward to the Mediterranean Sea on the west and to the Jordan River Valley and Dead Sea on the east. If you approach Jerusalem from either of these directions, you physically ascend.

Additionally, the temple was built on the top of Mount Moriah, where Abraham sacrificed Isaac. So to go to the temple from any part of Jerusalem, you would also ascend.

And thirdly, worshippers had to ascend stairs to get up to the platform that held the temple. As they climbed, they recited these psalms to prepare their hearts for worship.

All the psalms are short this week. (All psalms are short compared to Psalm 119.) With the exception of Psalm 132, all the songs of ascents are under ten verses. Some are as short as three verses, so we'll be covering two or three psalms each day.

Let's start by reading Psalm 120 and marking key words. What is the psalmist's situation? What does he request?

Now read and mark Psalm 121. What did you learn about God?

Record themes for Psalms 120 and 121 on PSALMS AT A GLANCE.

DAY TWO

Read Psalm 122, marking the key words as usual. List what you learned about Jerusalem. What are we to do for Jerusalem? Why? What will the result be?

Now read Psalm 123 and mark the key words from your bookmark. What does the psalmist say he will do toward God? Why? What does he request?

Record themes for Psalms 122 and 123 on PSALMS AT A GLANCE.

DAY THREE

Two more ascent psalms today. Read Psalm 124 and mark the key words from your bookmark. What did God do for Israel? What would have happened if God had not been on their side?

Now read and mark Psalm 125. What is true of those who trust in the Lord? What does the psalmist ask the Lord to do?

Record themes for Psalms 124 and 125 on PSALMS AT A GLANCE.

DAY FOUR

We'll look at three more ascent psalms today. Start with Psalm 126, reading and marking as before. Again, what has the Lord done for Israel? What does the psalmist request?

Now read and mark Psalm 127. What two subjects are covered? What is the main thought of each?

Finally, read and mark Psalm 128. Who is blessed and why? What are the blessings?

Now record themes for Psalms 126, 127, and 128 on PSALMS AT A GLANCE.

DAY FIVE

Three more short psalms of ascent today. Our first is Psalm 129. Read it, marking key words from your bookmark. What has the Lord done for Israel? What does the psalmist ask God to do for Israel?

Next is Psalm 130. Follow the usual pattern of marking. What does the psalmist ask of God?

What does he say he does toward the Lord? And what does he ask Israel to do?

The last psalm for today is Psalm 131 (just three verses). How does the psalmist describe himself and what he does, and what does he want Israel to do?

Finally, record themes for Psalms 129, 130, and 131 on PSALMS AT A GLANCE.

DAY SIX

Three psalms again today. The first is average length and the last two are just three verses each.

Read and mark Psalm 132 as usual.

What does the psalmist ask the Lord to remember? What event does he recall? (Hint: Note the key word in verse 8.) We've seen Psalms 96 and 105, which were written about this same event, but they don't mention the historical detail this psalm does. If you don't recall, go back to week 16, day 5, and week 18, days 1 and 2.

What is the psalmist's point in this psalm? What does he ask God to do and why?

Now read Psalm 133, marking key words. What is the main point of this short psalm?

Finally, our last psalm of ascents, Psalm 134. Read it and mark the key words from your bookmark. What is the main point of this psalm? Who is encouraged to do what?

Now record themes for Psalm 132, 133, and 134 on PSALMS AT A GLANCE.

DAY SEVEN

 Store in your heart: Psalm 122:6

Read and discuss: Psalms 120–134

Questions for Discussion or Individual Study

∽ Discuss the themes that run through these psalms—truths we are to know and how you can apply them.

∽ How do these psalms prepare a worshipper to go to the temple? Again, you can discuss this psalm by psalm.

∽ What have you learned from the songs of ascents? How will they impact your life? What truths will affect your relationship with God? What lessons will you commit to live out?

Thought for the Week

Where do you turn for help? I suppose you'll first ask, "Help in doing *what*?" We routinely do many things that we don't even think about asking for help with. For example, if someone asked you to add two small numbers, you'd give the answer without asking for help because you know how to do it.

This past week, we found a series of problems the psalmists asked God for help with. They were beyond their ability, problems like rescue from liars. You can't stop a liar from lying, and his lies can set snares that cause you all kinds of trouble.

And there are very good reasons to turn to God for help. As Creator, He has all the power needed to help. And as a God who cares about you, He has the desire to help. As the God who never slumbers or sleeps, He is always available to help. Because of His character—He is loving, merciful, just, faithful, and more—He *will* help.

The authors of these psalms (including David and Solomon) set an example of calling to God for help with a number of issues. They show us the kinds of things that we should call on God to help with. And they demonstrate trust in Him, recognizing their inabilities and His ultimate ability. Acknowledging these things is an act of worship.

But calling on God for help is related to another vital aspect of our relationship with God. We also learn the things we are to do to worship Him and obey His commands and statutes, as we saw in Psalm 119. We see examples like David in Psalm 122, who was glad when he went to the house of the Lord. We should go to God's house with this attitude. And David gives us instructions to obey that lead to acts of worship, like praying for the peace of Jerusalem.

Sometimes we need someone like David to remind us of what the Lord has done for us. If we forget, we can become independent. If we remember, we are more likely to place our trust in Him.

The songs of ascents show us how to worship (as other psalms do). From them we learn to sing (even shout) with joy and bless the Lord. We learn how to live our lives worshipping. We learn that children are a blessing and that dwelling in unity is good and pleasant.

If we trust God to answer in His ways, ways that are best for us, we wait and hope expectantly. Expectant waiting and hope are essential qualities for the Christian. The psalmists were waiting expectantly for the Messiah's coming. They hoped for deliverance. We too should wait expectantly, looking for the Lord's return.

SEARCH ME, O GOD, AND KNOW MY HEART

ᴄᴠᴄᴠᴄᴠᴄᴠ

Too often we hide our hearts from others and try to hide them from God. Only a humble person can honestly ask God to search and know his heart. He must know God can do this—search the heart and know it. And he must be willing to deal with whatever God finds there that needs changing. We always have some sin to repent of, some righteous behavior to practice.

ᴄᴠᴄᴠ

DAY ONE

Read Psalm 135 today, marking key words from your bookmark as you have been doing. List what you learned about praising God. Also list what you learned about idols and about God, and contrast the two. Compare your list today with the list you made from Psalm 115 on day 6 of week 19.

The house of Aaron is the priesthood. The house of Levi includes the house of Aaron and the other Levites who help with the temple service.

Record a theme for Psalm 135 on PSALMS AT A GLANCE.

DAY TWO

Read Psalm 136 and mark key words and phrases as usual. The most repeated phrase is pretty obvious since it occurs in every verse. So the key to this psalm is to list all the things God is and does.

Record a theme for Psalm 136 on PSALMS AT A GLANCE.

DAY THREE

We'll cover two psalms today. First, read Psalm 137 and mark the key words from your bookmark.

The kingdom of Israel split into two parts after the reign of Solomon. The southern kingdom, Judah, consisted mainly of Judah and Benjamin, though some from the other tribes remained faithful to worship God at His temple in Jerusalem. Babylon took Judah captive in three stages (605, 597, and 586 BC) and destroyed Jerusalem and its temple in 586 BC.

Where does this psalm take place? Why do the people weep? What two actions does the psalm call for?

Now read and mark Psalm 138. What did you learn about God? Who will worship God? Why will David worship Him? Why will the kings of the earth worship God?

Record themes for Psalms 137 and 138 on PSALMS AT A GLANCE.

DAY FOUR

Read Psalm 139 and mark the key words from your bookmark as usual. Then list what you learned about God. What truths from verses 13-16 did you learn about the unborn?

Finally, record a theme for Psalm 139 on PSALMS AT A GLANCE.

DAY FIVE

We're going to cover two psalms today. Begin by reading Psalm 140 and marking the key words from your bookmark. What did you learn about God? What did you learn about David's relationship with God? What does David ask God to do?

Now read Psalm 141 and mark key words. Answer the same questions about this psalm: What did you learn about God? What did you learn about David's relationship with God? What does David ask God to do?

Finally, record a theme for Psalms 140 and 141 on PSALMS AT A GLANCE.

DAY SIX

For the last day this week, we'll cover two psalms again. The first will be Psalm 142. Read it and mark key words according to the pattern we've followed for so many weeks.

This is another psalm by David. This time we know the setting—he was in a cave, hiding from Saul, who was trying to kill him. The same questions we asked yesterday will work for both psalms this week too: What did you learn about God? What did you learn about David's relationship with God? What does David ask God to do?

The second psalm for today is Psalm 143. Mark key words and phrases and answer the same questions as above.

Finally, record themes for Psalms 142 and 143 on PSALMS AT A GLANCE.

DAY SEVEN

 Store in your heart: Psalm 139:23-24
Read and discuss: Psalms 135–143

QUESTIONS FOR DISCUSSION OR INDIVIDUAL STUDY

- ∾ Discuss what you learned about God this week.

- ∾ Also discuss what you learned about David and his heart this week from Psalms 138–143.

- ∾ Discuss how the lovingkindness of the Lord relates to His wonderful deeds.

- ∾ What did you learn about your relationship to God when you were in the womb?

- ∾ Discuss what God knows about you.

- ∾ What have you learned from these psalms that will impact your life? What truths will affect your relationship with God? What lessons will you commit to live out?

THOUGHT FOR THE WEEK

Did you ever watch the television series called *Home Improvement?* The story was about a man who had a television program called *Tool Time.* He used tools to fix different things in the home, but inevitably in each episode he also learned something about his wife and children that "fixed" something else—their relationships and consequently their home life. So the title *Home Improvement* had two meanings.

What brings this illustration to mind is the idea from this week's psalms that there is always need for improvement in our lives. Things are never perfect. Our hearts are home to the Holy Spirit, who dwells in us, and *that* home needs improvement too.

David was bold in Psalm 139. He asked God to search and know his heart. He wanted God to reveal to him hurtful ways within. And he wanted God to lead him in the everlasting way. Is that your desire too? Do you want God to reveal what you need to improve, to lead you in the everlasting way? Or do you want to leave things just as they are?

If you don't want God to help you improve your home for the Holy Spirit, why not? What does that reveal about your relationship with God? The interesting thing is that God already knows what needs improvement. David asked that God would reveal what needed to change. That's what we should ask for too.

Hebrews 4:12 tells us something very powerful about the Scripture: "For the word of God is living and active and sharper than any two-edged sword, and piercing as far as the division of soul and spirit, of both joints and marrow, and able to judge the thoughts and intentions of the heart" (Hebrews 4:12).

This is crucial to Bible study. When we come to the Word

of God we must know that it will judge the thoughts and intentions of our hearts. So when we study, we should have the same desire David had to have God search and know our hearts and show us our self-destructive ways.

Second Timothy 3:16-17 tells us that all Scripture is God-breathed and useful to instruct us in where we've gone astray. It shows us how to return to God and train ourselves to be everything God intended us to be. The key is that Scripture has that power. Reading the Word of God is unlike reading other books. Only the Scripture has the power to judge our thoughts and intentions, show us what's wrong and how to correct it, and train us in how to live so we can be all that God intended.

When we fail to grasp the supernatural power of God's Word itself, we end up turning to man's word—man's books about God, about the Bible, about life and how to live it. And if we do this instead of reading our Bibles, we miss the encounter with God that He intended when He inspired biblical writers. We miss the transforming power of God's holy Word.

Even devotional studies like this one are no substitute for God's Word. But you already know that because you've done six days of study in Psalms this week before you got this far (I hope!). You've had 23 weeks of encountering God and His precious Word piercing your heart. You already know it has turned up warts and wrinkles and things that need fixing. You've seen how this tool, the Word, improves the Holy Spirit's home.

If this is the first book in the New Inductive Study Series you've used to study the Bible, why not get the whole set? God wrote 66 books of the Bible, and He intended for us to read all 66. Each book includes God's revelation of Himself and more opportunities for us to expose ourselves to His tool for measuring us, trying us, showing us what needs improving, and helping us change and grow.

Dig in to the whole counsel of God. Mine the treasures that are within, plumb the depths of the truths that God has recorded through His faithful servants, and let every nook and cranny, every corner of your heart be exposed to the light of God's Word. And then clean house, fix up what needs repair, and redecorate if you need to, to make the inside pure and holy. Then your outward behavior will reflect the inside changes, and God will be glorified.

Press on, Beloved. Press on.

What Is Man, That You Take Knowledge of Him?

We're pretty insignificant compared to God. We're like a mere breath, and our days are a passing shadow. But according to Genesis we were created in His image, and no other part of His creation has this distinction. So something about man is special in God's creation. Many psalms call all creation to praise the Lord, but man has a unique God-consciousness and ability to articulate praise to Him.

DAY ONE

Read Psalm 144 today, marking key words from your bookmark as you have been doing. Make a list of what you learned about God, and then record a theme for Psalm 144 on PSALMS AT A GLANCE.

DAY TWO

Today we'll study Psalm 145. Read it, mark the key words, and then list what you learned about God.

Record a theme for Psalm 145 on PSALMS AT A GLANCE.

DAY THREE

Read Psalm 146 today and mark the key words from your bookmark. List reasons you should praise the Lord—truths about Him.

Record a theme for Psalm 146 on PSALMS AT A GLANCE.

DAY FOUR

Psalm 147 is our subject for study today. Follow the usual pattern for marking and listing what you learned about God. What is the distinction between Israel and other nations?

Finally, record a theme for Psalm 147 on PSALMS AT A GLANCE.

DAY FIVE

Read Psalm 148 and mark the key words from your bookmark. List who and what should praise the Lord and why they should.

Finally, record a theme for Psalm 148 on PSALMS AT A GLANCE.

DAY SIX

Our last day of study together. God will honor your

perseverance! Two more psalms, and we've reached our goal of 150 psalms. First read Psalm 149 and mark key words as we have been doing now for 24 weeks of study.

Again, who should rejoice and be glad in God? What honor does God give His godly ones?

Now read our last psalm (number 150) and mark the key words. List the things you learned in this psalm about praising God. Use the 5W's and an H.

Finally, record themes for Psalms 149 and 150 on PSALMS AT A GLANCE.

DAY SEVEN

Store in your heart: Psalm 144:3
Read and discuss: Psalms 144–150

QUESTIONS FOR DISCUSSION OR INDIVIDUAL STUDY

- Discuss all you learned this week about praising God. Use the 5 W's and an H.

- Discuss what you learned about God.

- What special benefits did Israel receive as God's chosen people?

- What special relationship does man have with God?

- Spend some time summarizing some of the main things you've learned from Psalms.

- Share your favorite verses.

- What have you learned from this study of Psalms that will impact your life? What truths will affect your relationship with God? What lessons will you commit to live out?

THOUGHT FOR THE WEEK

If I asked you to sum up our 24 weeks studying Psalms, what would you say is the central message of the whole book? We've seen a distressed David pour out his heart to God for deliverance from his enemies. Is this the main idea?

We've seen psalms that request God to judge righteously, destroy the wicked, and vindicate the righteous; others declare His greatness, character, ways, and deeds; still others praise and thank Him. Are any of these the main theme?

Or would it be that God thinks about man, does things on his behalf, and asks man to acknowledge these things? God tells us to acknowledge His care for us. How? By coming to Him when we need help. By thanking Him for what He has done for us. By singing His praises to Him, to other believers, and to the world. By declaring truth about Him to all the world, so everyone knows He cares.

That's what psalms do. They declare God's greatness and praise Him. All through this study we've directed you to list what you learned about God. What you know about God is really the only basis on which you can praise God. You and I have not experienced everything God has done. The psalms recount unique experiences Israel had that we haven't.

We know God through these recorded experiences even if we haven't lived them. We learn of His mighty works of old. We experience His love and faithfulness, but we never experience all He has done in and for all those who have trusted Him. We learn their stories and the principles of trusting God that come with them. Everything we need to know to praise God properly is contained in His Word. The psalms are expressions of faith and trust in Him. We can develop this faith and trust using the psalmists' words.

God's relationship to man is special. His revelation of Himself to man is part of that special relationship. Regardless of how flawed our human relationships are, God's love for us is perfect. He expresses that love partly by revealing Himself and His ways to us. Our side of the relationship isn't perfect, but God's is. Even though our obedience is imperfect, we can worship and praise God for what He has done for us.

God's intention in creating man, male and female, in His image, was to bring Himself glory. According to the Westminster Shorter Catechism, "Man's chief end is to glorify God and enjoy Him forever." To glorify Him we must appreciate His attributes and deeds. We must adore and worship Him. Scripture details appropriate ways to worship God so we don't "do our own thing." The point of worship is to do *His* thing.

When God gave Israel the law at Mount Sinai, He detailed worship, answering all the 5 W's and an H questions His people could ask about worship. One day, two sons of Aaron the high priest, Nadab and Abihu, offered "strange fire before the Lord, which He had not commanded them." Fire came out from the presence of the Lord and consumed them. The priests could not draw near to God and honor Him before all the people if they were willful and disobedient. They were required to treat God as holy.

This principle of treating God as holy has not changed. Peter wrote in his first letter that we are to offer sacrifices *acceptable* to God. In order for our worship to be acceptable, it must conform to God's standards. It must not only show our appreciation and adoration of Him but also reflect our true affection for Him. We must truly love Him with all our heart, mind, soul, and strength. That's not the same thing as acting as if we love Him; it must be genuine.

Finally, to treat God as holy, to worship Him acceptably, we must subject ourselves to Him. He rules, and we must obey. This is why living is part of worship. Too often today in our congregations we tend to limit worship to singing. The problem with this is that the Scripture teaches that music is not all there is to worship. Without the love and obedience God demands, it's just music even if the words are praises. In other words, if our lives don't reflect the words we're singing, we're not authentically worshipping.

We can use the psalms as patterns for our worship. We can learn the principles of living under the sovereignty of God and lordship of Jesus Christ. Then we can live out these principles—singing our praise, yes, but also living our praise.

Now go praise the Lord and glorify Him with all your being and life!

SEGMENT DIVISIONS

			CHAPTER THEMES
		1	Wicked v. righteous man
		2	
		3	
		4	
		5	
		6	
		7	
		8	
		9	
		10	
		11	
		12	
		13	
		14	
		15	
		16	
		17	
		18	
		19	
		20	
		21	
		22	
		23	
		24	
		25	

Author:

Date:

Geographical Location:

Purpose:

Key Words (and their synonyms):

affliction

take refuge

righteous

wicked

sin (iniquity)

prayer

praise

sing

fear

hope

save

cry

SEGMENT DIVISIONS

		CHAPTER THEMES
		26
		27
		28
		29
		30
		31
		32
		33
		34
		35
		36
		37
		38
		39
		40
		41
		42
		43
		44
		45
		46
		47
		48
		49
		50

SEGMENT DIVISIONS

			CHAPTER THEMES
		51	
		52	
		53	
		54	
		55	
		56	
		57	
		58	
		59	
		60	
		61	
		62	
		63	
		64	
		65	
		66	
		67	
		68	
		69	
		70	
		71	
		72	
		73	
		74	
		75	

SEGMENT DIVISIONS

			CHAPTER THEMES
		76	
		77	
		78	
		79	
		80	
		81	
		82	
		83	
		84	
		85	
		86	
		87	
		88	
		89	
		90	
		91	
		92	
		93	
		94	
		95	
		96	
		97	
		98	
		99	
		100	

SEGMENT DIVISIONS

		CHAPTER THEMES
		101
		102
		103
		104
		105
		106
		107
		108
		109
		110
		111
		112
		113
		114
		115
		116
		117
		118
		119
		120
		121
		122
		123
		124
		125

			CHAPTER THEMES
		126	
		127	
		128	
		129	
		130	
		131	
		132	
		133	
		134	
		135	
		136	
		137	
		138	
		139	
		140	
		141	
		142	
		143	
		144	
		145	
		146	
		147	
		148	
		149	
		150	

Notes

1. KJV, NKJV: ungodly
2. KJV, NKJV: shout
3. KJV, NKJV, NIV: mercy; ESV: steadfast love
4. NIV: wrong; ESV: evildoers
5. NIV: sins
6. KJV: vexed; NKJV: troubled; NIV: in agony; ESV: troubled
7. KJV, NKJV: just
8. NIV: abhor
9. KJV, NKJV: pavilion; NIV: dwelling; ESV: shelter
10. KJV, NKVJ, ESV: give; NIV: repay
11. KJV: desert; NKJV, NIV: deserve; ESV: due reward
12. KJV, NKJV, ESV: cast down; NIV: downcast
13. ESV: ransom
14. NIV, ESV: ransom
15. KJV: trusteth; NKJV: trusts
16. KJV, NKJV: mercy; NIV: loving; ESV: steadfast love
17. KJV, NKJV: dishonor; NIV: dishonor, scorn, insult; ESV: dishonor
18. NIV: God Almighty
19. NIV: decrees
20. KJV, NKJV: judgments; NIV: laws; ESV: rules
21. NIV: laws; ESV: rules

Books in the
New Inductive Study Series

❧❧❧❧❧

CHANGING THE WAY
PEOPLE STUDY GOD'S WORD

"Inductive study of the Bible is the best way to discover scriptural truth... There is no jewel more precious than that which you have mined yourself."

—HOWARD HENDRICKS

Every feature is designed to help you gain a more intimate understanding of God and His Word. This study Bible, the only one based entirely on the inductive study approach, provides you with the tools for observing what the text says, interpreting what it means, and applying it to your life.